DISCOVERING
SCOTLAND'S
LOST RAILWAYS

CAPTIONS TO PRELIMS SECTION

Half-title: *The end of the line at Loch Tay engine shed in August 1965. BR Standard Class 4 2-6-4 tank No. 80093 is coaled and watered less than two months before this delightful branch line from Killin Junction closed.*

Title: *North of Appin the trackbed of the Connel Ferry to Ballachulish branch hugs the eastern shore of Loch Linnhe, where there are fine views of privately owned Shuna Island and the mountains beyond.*

Contents: *'B1' 4-6-0 No. 61330 enters Cameron Bridge on the Fife coast line with the two-coach 2.42pm Crail to Thornton Junction train on 6 August 1965.*

Introduction: *At nearly ¾-mile long, Whitrope Tunnel on the Waverley Route is the fourth-longest railway tunnel in Scotland. Access is now barred by a metal fence due to a roof collapse at the southern end in 2002.*

DISCOVERING
SCOTLAND'S
LOST RAILWAYS

WAVERLEY
BOOKS

JULIAN HOLLAND

Published by Waverley Books, 144 Port Dundas Road, Glasgow, G4 0HZ, Scotland.

Conceived, designed and written by Julian Holland.

© Waverley Books 2009
Text © Julian Holland 2009
Photographs © Julian Holland 2009
First published 2009, reprinted 2010

The publishers gratefully acknowledge the help of the Museum of Transport, Glasgow and the Scottish Railway Preservation Society, and Colin Campbell and Tony Jervis for their editorial input.

A catalogue record for this book is available from the British Library.

ISBN 978-1-902407-80-7
Printed and bound in Poland

The contents of this book are believed correct at the time of printing. Nevertheless, the publishers cannot accept responsibility for errors or omissions, or for changes in details given.

CONTENTS

INTRODUCTION

The mid-to-late 19th century was a boom period for railway building in Scotland. Many lines were built, often through sparsely populated areas and with unrealistic forecasts for a bright future. Some schemes never even saw the light of day and if they had been built would never have paid a return to their financial backers. Classic examples of these failed schemes include many in northwest Scotland which sought to profit from the fishing industry – if the Highland Railway had had its way there would have been railways serving Aultbea, Ullapool and Lochinver and light railways on the islands of Skye and Lewis. None of these schemes saw the light of day.

Uneconomic railways were being closed in Scotland many years before Dr Beeching arrived on the scene. Prior to the nationalisation of the railways in 1948 casualties included the narrow gauge Campbeltown & Machrihanish Light Railway on the Kintyre Penisula (closed 1932), Wick & Lybster Light Railway (closed 1944) and the Spean Bridge to Fort Augustus line (closed to passengers in 1933 and completely in 1946).

Railway closures in Scotland gathered pace in the early 1950s after the British Transport Commission formed the 'Branch Lines Committee'. While freight services were still retained many lightly used lines soon lost their passenger services – among the long list of closures in 1951 was the scenic line from Comrie to Balquhidder alongside Loch Earn and branches to Fortrose and Macduff.

If fully implemented, Dr Beeching's 1963 report 'The Reshaping of British Railways' would have left enormous tracts of Scotland without a rail service. Even so, by the end of the 1960s the railway map of Scotland had shrunk considerably with the closure of lines in Speyside, northeast Aberdeenshire, the Dee Valley, Perthshire, Galloway, the Borders and along the Fife and Morayshire coasts. Gone too was the Ballachulish branch and the eastern half of the Callander & Oban line. Fortunately both public and political pressure saved the lines in the far north to Wick and Thurso, to Kyle of Lochalsh and between Ayr and Stranraer.

Less well known is Dr Beeching's second report 'The Development of the Major Railway Trunk Routes' which was published in 1964. This would have seen the closure of all lines in Scotland apart from those along the Carlisle – Glasgow – Edinburgh – Perth – Aberdeen corridor. Fortunately, by this time, the political scene had changed and the report was not implemented.

The world has changed a lot since the 1960s and the future of railways in Scotland is looking much more positive. Several closed lines in the central belt have recently been reopened and the 35-mile northern section of the Waverley Route from Edinburgh to Tweedbank is due to reopen in 2013. Others might follow – watch this space!

This then is the background to Scotland's lost railways. They may be gone but they are not forgotten. Built to last by their Victorian and Edwardian engineers much of their infrastructure is still in place – new life for redundant station buildings; cycleways and footpaths following the old trackbeds, embankments and cuttings; graceful steel bridges spanning the rivers; soaring viaducts striding across the landscape and burrowing tunnels beneath it. Much of Scotland's lost railway heritage is still out there waiting to be discovered.

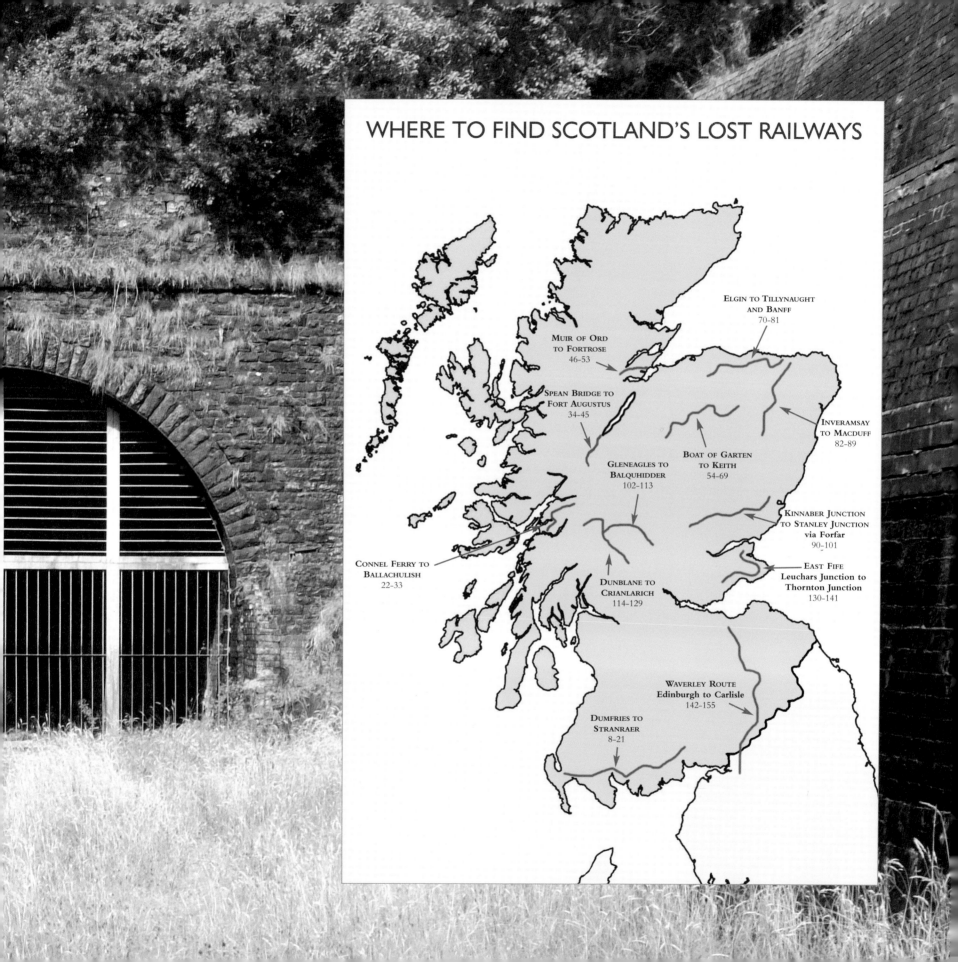

WHERE TO FIND SCOTLAND'S LOST RAILWAYS

ELGIN TO TILLYNAUGHT
AND BANFF
70–81

MUIR OF ORD
TO FORTROSE
46–53

SPEAN BRIDGE TO
FORT AUGUSTUS
34–45

INVERAMSAY
TO MACDUFF
82–89

BOAT OF GARTEN
TO KEITH
54–69

GLENEAGLES TO
BALQUHIDDER
102–113

KINNABER JUNCTION
TO STANLEY JUNCTION
via Forfar
90–101

CONNEL FERRY TO
BALLACHULISH
22–33

EAST FIFE
Leuchars Junction to
Thornton Junction
130–141

DUNBLANE TO
CRIANLARICH
114–129

WAVERLEY ROUTE
Edinburgh to Carlisle
142–155

DUMFRIES TO
STRANRAER
8–21

DUMFRIES TO STRANRAER

The shortest sea crossing from Britain to Ireland is the 21-mile wide channel between Portpatrick in southwest Scotland and Donaghadee in County Down, Northern Ireland. However, with the opening of the Chester to Holyhead railway in 1850, the majority of traffic across the Irish Sea, including the all-important Irish mail, was being transported via the Holyhead to Dublin route. To seize back some of this lost traffic, various railway proposals were put forward to link Portpatrick to the expanding rail network in Scotland. The first stage of a railway across Galloway began in 1859 with the opening of the Castle Douglas & Dumfries Railway. This was followed in 1861 by the opening of the section from Castle Douglas to Stranraer with the final steeply graded line to Portpatrick being completed a year later.

Meanwhile, the Ayr & Maybole Railway had opened in 1856 and the Maybole & Girvan Railway in 1860. The missing link, the Girvan & Portpatrick Junction Railway, between Girvan and Challoch Junction on the Portpatrick Railway, was opened in 1877.

Working the steeply graded line down to the little harbour at Portpatrick was never easy, and in 1874 all ferry traffic was diverted to a new terminal at Stranraer which connected to Larne, the railway-linked port in Ireland. The line to Portpatrick then reverted to branch-line status and finally closed in 1950.

The next twist in this tale came in 1885 when the Castle Douglas to Stranraer and Portpatrick line, including a branch from Newton Stewart to Whithorn, was amalgamated into the Portpatrick & Wigtownshire Joint Railway and run jointly by four major players – the London & North Western, the Midland, the Caledonian and the Glasgow & South Western Railways (G&SWR). Trains were

Left *Northwest of Castle Douglas, the rusting bridge over Loch Ken is now too dangerous for pedestrians or vehicles. Blocked on the east by a high metal gate, the western side is reached by road on a 10-mile detour via New Galloway.*

Below *The once-busy Glasgow & South Western Railway main line from Glasgow St Enoch to Gretna Junction via Dumfries is now served by First ScotRail. Although the roof girders still remain, the bay for Stranraer-line trains at Dumfries has now been filled in.*

Carlisle, northeast England and London. Although local traffic was always light in this sparsely populated region of Galloway the railway was heavily used during World War II. After nationalisation in 1948 the railway remained an important route for cattle and troop trains and the nightly 'The Northern Irishman' sleeping car train (known as 'The Paddy') between London Euston and Stranraer Harbour. Additionally, during the summer months the 'Stranraer to Larne Boat Train' ran on Saturday nights from Newcastle to Stranraer Harbour. Local stopping trains from Dumfries usually terminated at Stranraer Town station.

By the early 1960s the writing was on the wall for this scenic route and by the summer of 1964, apart from the two scheduled overnight boat trains, there were only three scheduled passenger trains each way between Dumfries and Stranraer. Steam-hauled to the end, the line between Dumfries and Challoch Junction was closed on 14 June 1965 and Stranraer Harbour boat trains were diverted via Mauchline and Ayr. Despite the early introduction of diesel multiple units on the Stranraer Harbour to Glasgow route, steam continued to be seen until October 1966 when the Stranraer engine shed closed. Fortunately Stranraer Harbour is still served by passenger trains from Glasgow today.

Above *Seen here on 1 September 1954, Dumfries engine shed (BR code 68B/67E) provided much of the motive power for trains on the Stranraer line. Ex-LMS types allocated here included 2P 4-4-0s and Stanier 'Black Five' 4-6-0s. The shed closed to steam in May 1966 and has since been demolished.*

Below *BR Standard Class 4 2-6-0 No. 76072 pauses at Dalbeattie with a Dumfries to Stranraer stopping train on 8 June 1963. Only seven years old when photographed here, No. 76072 was built at Doncaster and withdrawn from Dumfries shed in October 1964.*

worked jointly by the Caledonian and the G&SWR with the latter company also taking over the Castle Douglas & Dumfries Railway.
On the Ayrshire coast the route from Ayr down to Stranraer via Girvan became part of the G&SWR in 1892.

The two routes to Stranraer then settled down to co-exist together and were both absorbed into the newly formed London, Midland & Scotland Railway (LMS) in 1923. The northerly route, via Girvan and Ayr, carried freight and passenger traffic to and from Glasgow, while the route via Castle Douglas and Dumfries saw traffic to and from

THE LINE TODAY

Armed with Ordnance Survey Landranger Maps 82, 83, 84 much of the route of this closed railway line can be followed today by a combination of car, bicycle and foot. Of note is the well-preserved goods shed in an industrial estate at Castle Douglas, the rusting and slighly menacing girder bridge over Loch Ken, the section of trackbed west of New Galloway station that is now designated the 'Kite Trail' and which continues along Forestry Commission tracks for several miles to the imposing Big Water of Fleet Viaduct. Little Gatehouse of Fleet station (7 miles from the village of that name) is now a private residence while a short section of trackbed north of Creetown is now part of Sustrans National Cycle Network (NCN) Route 7. West of Newton Stewart the old railway disappears for a while due to road improvements to the A75 but by Kirkcowan the cuttings, embankments and bridges are clearly defined. The tall and graceful Glenluce Viaduct is a fitting end to the memory of this long-lamented railway line.

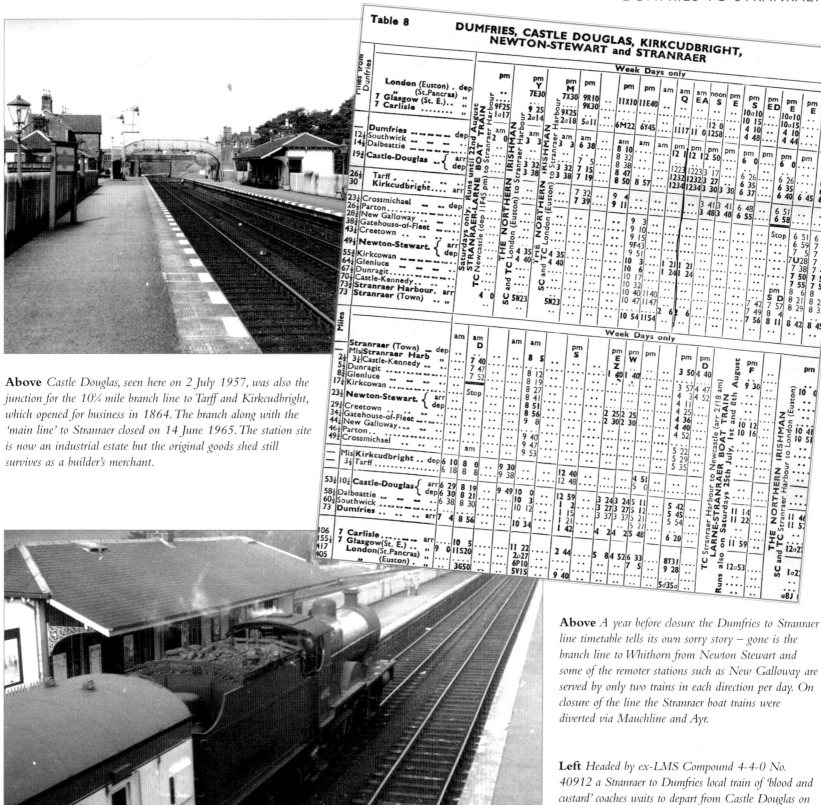

Above *Castle Douglas, seen here on 2 July 1957, was also the junction for the 10¼ mile branch line to Tarff and Kirkcudbright, which opened for business in 1864. The branch along with the 'main line' to Stranraer closed on 14 June 1965. The station site is now an industrial estate but the original goods shed still survives as a builder's merchant.*

Above *A year before closure the Dumfries to Stranraer line timetable tells its own sorry story – gone is the branch line to Whithorn from Newton Stewart and some of the remoter stations such as New Galloway are served by only two trains in each direction per day. On closure of the line the Stranraer boat trains were diverted via Mauchline and Ayr.*

Left *Headed by ex-LMS Compound 4-4-0 No. 40912 a Stranraer to Dumfries local train of 'blood and custard' coaches waits to depart from Castle Douglas on 16 April 1953. Allocated to Dumfries engine shed, this engine was built at the Vulcan Foundry, Lancashire, in 1927 and withdrawn in April 1955.*

Above *A short passenger train headed by a 'Black Five' 4-6-0 coasts across the Loch Ken bridge two months before the complete closure of the line in June 1965.*

Below *Although the growth of trees has now obstructed the former railway embankment, holidaymakers at the Parton camping and caravan site still have a fine view of the Loch Ken bridge from the eastern shore of the loch.*

Below *The Loch Ken bridge viewed from the western side of the loch. The sign clearly warns of the risks of crossing. It's now hard to imagine 'The Northern Irishman' with its sleeping cars headed by a 'Black Five' or 'Clan' Pacific rumbling over this bridge in the dead of night.*

Right *A Dumfries to Stranraer train rumbles away from the Loch Ken bridge as it approaches New Galloway station on 2 July 1957. Waiting for the single line token is a Stranraer to Dumfries boat train of 'blood and custard' coaches double-headed by an ex-LMS Compound 4-4-0 and a Stanier 'Black Five' 4-6-0.*

Left *The view of New Galloway station today is much obscured by vegetation but the platform edge has been revealed by the local owner. By the 1960s only two trains a day in each direction stopped here and, since it was also over 4 miles from the village it purported to serve, it is hardly surprising that locally generated traffic was light.*

Above *The trackbed west of New Galloway station is now dedicated as the 'Kite Trail' – a popular location for birdwatchers to spot the rare red kite. Five miles further west lies the remote remains of Loch Skerrow Halt, where steam trains once paused to top up their water supply. Beyond Loch Skerrow the trackbed follows Forestry Commission tracks to the imposing Big Water of Fleet Viaduct.*

Left and below *The imposing 20-arch viaduct over the Big Water of Fleet was built in 1861 but heavy wartime traffic wrought its toll on the structure. By 1924 cracks had started to appear in the masonry and the ugly brick casing around the piers and tie rods were added as reinforcements.*

Above *With only two months to go before the closure of the line from Dumfries, a Stranraer-bound mixed freight train headed by a Stanier 'Black Five' crosses the Big Water of Fleet Viaduct in April 1965. The viaduct is now owned by Sustrans, whose NCN Route 7 passes beneath the structure.*

Above *The highest point on the Dumfries to Stranraer line was Gatehouse of Fleet station which was located 7 miles northwest from the small town it served. The attractive station building is now a private residence.*

Left *In April 1965, a filthy and uncared-for 'Black Five' 4-6-0 hauls an eastbound goods train from Stranraer through a lonely Gatehouse of Fleet station.*

Right *The single-storey station building at Newton Stewart on 23 March 1963. This station was the junction for the 19¼-mile branch line to Whithorn, which opened as the Wigtownshire Railway between 1875 and 1877. It soon fell on hard times and was amalgamated into the Portpatrick & Wigtownshire Joint Railway in 1885. The line closed to passengers in 1950 and to goods on 5 October 1964.*

Left *A 'Black Five' pauses at Newton Stewart with a Stranraer train in April 1965. Latterly, Newton Stewart was served by just four trains a day in each direction, one of which was 'The Northern Irishman' overnight sleeper train to and from London Euston.*

Below *Veteran ex-Caledonian Railway Drummond 0-6-0 No. 57375 heads an enthusiasts special to the Whithorn branch at Newton Stewart in 1963. This beautifully turned-out loco was built at St Rollox Works in Glasgow in 1894 and withdrawn from Stranraer engine shed in November 1963.*

Above *Newton Stewart station on 21 June 1937. It's a bright summer's day and nothing much seems to be happening. The sidings on the left are full of cattle wagons – one of the staple goods of this line. As with many closed stations, the site is now an industrial estate but the goods and engine sheds still stand.*

Left *Kirkcowan station in the sunshine on 2 July 1957. Little remains of this site and even the road bridge in the background has been demolished. By 1964 this station was only served by two trains in each direction per day – one in the morning and one in the afternoon.*

Right *A mile to the east of Challoch Junction, where the Girvan line joined the Portpatrick & Wigtownshire Joint, lies Glenluce Viaduct. Its graceful arches span the fast-flowing Water of Luce, a favourite spot for fishermen. The site of Glenluce station disappeared long ago.*

Below *The end of the line at Stranraer Harbour. The once-busy freight sidings are silent now that everything is transported by road. The station here is still served by three trains each day to and from Glasgow.*

CONNEL FERRY TO BALLACHULISH

The Callander & Oban Railway Company (C&OR) was incorporated in 1865 to build a railway between those two towns. The scheme was supported by the Caledonian Railway (CR), which agreed to operate it provided it was more than 20 miles in length. However, the C&OR ran into financial problems before the railway was completed and had to be bailed out by the CR. The line to Oban finally opened in 1880 and a branch from Ballachulish was authorised in 1896 to carry slate from the Ballachulish quarries to the C&OR main line at Connel Ferry. The line, for much of its length, runs along the eastern shore of Loch Linnhe. Its construction by Robert McAlpine involved the building of two substantial bridges – one over Loch Etive at Connel Ferry and the other over Loch Creran at Creagan. The 27-mile branch line was opened on 24 August 1903, and for most of its life it was the haunt of ex-Caledonian Railway 0-4-4 passenger tanks and Drummond 0-6-0 freight locomotives.

A small halt and siding at Barcaldine, between Benderloch and Creagan, was opened in 1914.

By 1964 the end of the line was looming for the Ballachulish branch though it was still served by four trains each way per day - three of them departing from or terminating at Oban. Despite the introduction of diesels in its final years the line succumbed to 'the Beeching axe' and closed to goods on 14 June 1965 and to passengers on 28 March 1966. Although it was hastily dismantled there is much that still remains of the railway's infrastructure.

THE LINE TODAY

Connel Ferry station is still open on the Glasgow Queen Street to Oban line. By far the most impressive relic of the Ballachulish branch line, the cantilever bridge at Connel Ferry, now converted to

Left *Once a passing loop, Creagan station has recently been beautifully restored as a private residence. It is clearly visible from the A828 north of the Creagan bridge.*

Above *Road traffic waits for a train from Ballachulish to cross Connel Ferry Bridge on 19 April 1952. Until 1914 road vehicles were carried across the bridge to North Connel on a specially adapted goods wagon. The bridge was then resurfaced to accommodate both road and rail traffic.*

Left *Ex-Caledonian Railway McIntosh '812' 0-6-0 No. 57571 crosses Connel Bridge with a freight train from Ballachulish to Connel Ferry in September 1960. The asphalted road surface on the left was added in 1914 to allow road traffic to cross the bridge. Until the closure of the railway in 1966 road tolls were collected by British Railways.*

Freight traffic at Ballachulish was originally dominated by output from the local slate quarries, but in its latter years the Kinlochleven aluminium smelter (now closed) generated large volumes of inbound alumina and outbound aluminium by rail. A map in the 1963 Beeching Report showed Ballachulish goods station as falling into the highest of three national categories for freight, '25,000 tons and over per annum'.

Below *The major engineering feature on the Ballachulish branch was the rail bridge over Loch Etive at Connel Ferry. When completed in 1903 it was the second-largest cantilever bridge in the world – the largest at that time was the Forth Bridge. The bridge was designed by Sir John Wolfe Barry and built by Henry Marc Brunel, the second son of Isambard Kingdom Brunel. It now carries a single-track road.*

a single-track road bridge, crosses the tidal Falls of Lora. During the early years of the railway motor cars were carried across on a railway wagon to a platform at North Connel. In 1914 the bridge's surface was rebuilt to allow both cars and trains to cross. Part of the trackbed at Benderloch has been converted into an asphalted foot and cycle path.

The other major engineering structure on the line was the twin girder bridge across Loch Creran at Creagan. The bridge, which was fitted with a pedestrian walkway, remained in situ for more than 30 years after the line's closure and was only rebuilt as a road bridge at the end of the 20th century.

After crossing the bridge the route of the line can easily be seen to the right of the A828 – here there is a small railway overbridge and the beautifully restored Creagan station (now a private residence) complete with island platform, clock, original fencing, station building, nameboard and the base of the water tower. At Appin the route of the line is easily recognised as it heads up the Strath of Appin before bearing north along the eastern shore of Loch Linnhe. With views across the loch to the mountains high above Kingairloch on the western shore this must have been a spectacular journey during the days of the railway. The substantial station building at Duror is now a private residence while the station and platforms at Kentallen have been rebuilt as a hotel. The trackbed between here and the rock cuttings of South Ballachulish has been converted into an asphalted cycle path offering much-needed respite for cyclists from the dangerously fast and narrow A828. A reminder of the railway – a latticework distant semaphore signal – stands in a driveway close to the main road on the approach to Ballachulish. Here most of the station site has been redeveloped as a housing estate while the old station building is now a medical centre.

Above *Cheery waves at Benderloch on a wet and windy day on 19 April 1952. All of this has since vanished – except for the wind and the rain!*

Left *A short section of the trackbed at Benderloch has been resurfaced as a cycleway and footpath, providing walkers and cyclists with a safe alternative to the fast and dangerous A828.*

Below *Concrete was heavily used in the construction of the Ballachulish branch. This concrete bridge carries the lane to Barcaldine Castle over the trackbed of the railway between Benderloch and Barcaldine. You can see Loch Creran in the background.*

Above *Creagan Viaduct was completed in 1903 and carried the Ballachulish branch across a narrow channel of Loch Creran. The two old lattice steel spans remained in situ for more than 30 years following closure of the line in 1966. They were replaced in 1999 by this modern concrete structure which was built on the piers of the old bridge, reducing the road journey around the loch by 5½ miles.*

Left *To the north of Creagan Viaduct this concrete bridge carried the railway over a private drive. Pioneered by 'Concrete Bob' (Sir Robert McAlpine), concrete had become an important material in the construction of railways by the late 19th century.*

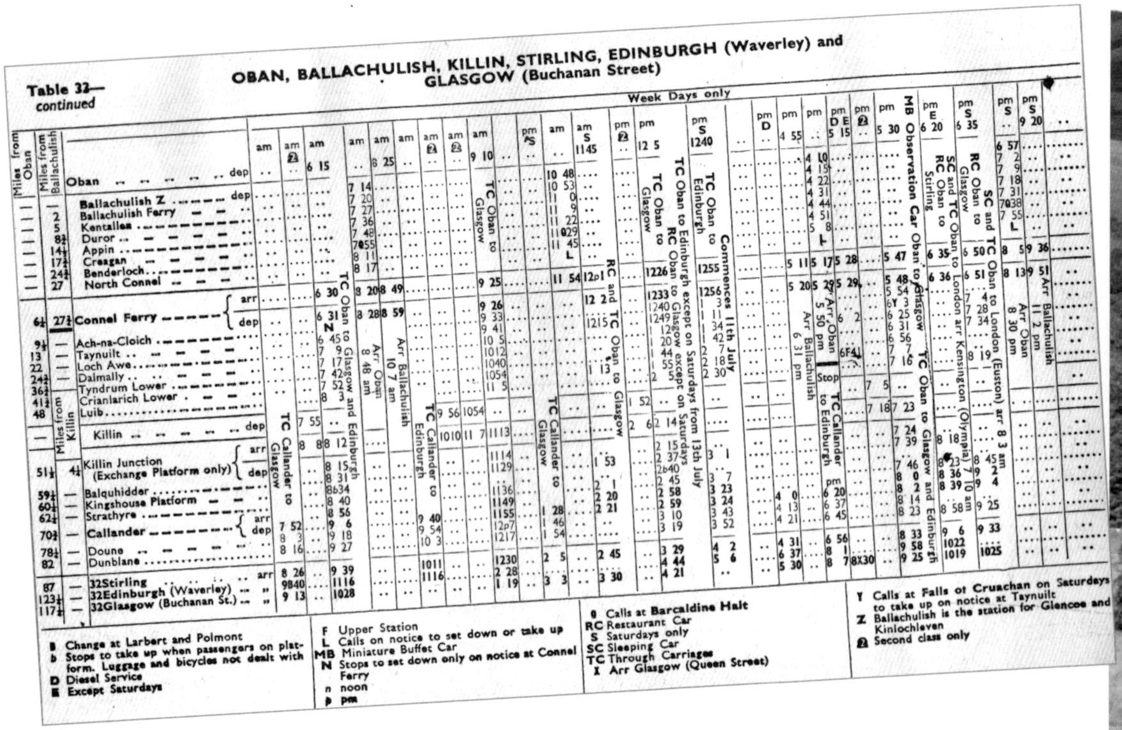

Table 32—
continued

OBAN, BALLACHULISH, KILLIN, STIRLING, EDINBURGH (Waverley) and GLASGOW (Buchanan Street)

Week Days only

Miles from Oban	Miles from Ballachulish	Station	
		Oban	dep
—	—	Ballachulish Z	dep
—	2	Ballachulish Ferry	
—	5	Kentallen	
—	8½	Duror	
—	14½	Appin	
—	17½	Creagan	
—	24½	Benderloch	
—	27	North Connel	
6½	27½	Connel Ferry	arr / dep
9½	—	Ach-na-Cloich	
13	—	Taynuilt	
22	—	Loch Awe	
24½	—	Dalmally	
36½		Tyndrum Lower	
41½		Crianlarich Lower	
48	Miles from Killin	Luib	
—		Killin	dep
51½	4½	Killin Junction (Exchange Platform only)	arr / dep
59½	—	Balquhidder	
60½	—	Kingshouse Platform	
62½	—	Strathyre	
70½	—	Callander	arr / dep
78½	—	Doune	
82	—	Dunblane	
87	—	32Stirling	arr
123½	—	32Edinburgh (Waverley)	"
117½	—	32Glasgow (Buchanan St.)	"

B Change at Larbert and Polmont
b Stops to take up when passengers on platform. Luggage and bicycles not dealt with
D Diesel Service
E Except Saturdays
F Upper Station
L Calls on notice to set down or take up
MB Miniature Buffet Car
N Stops to set down only on notice at Connel Ferry
n noon
p pm
θ Calls at Barcaldine Halt
RC Restaurant Car
S Saturdays only
SC Sleeping Car
TC Through Carriages
X Arr Glasgow (Queen Street)
Y Calls at Falls of Cruachan on Saturdays to take up on notice at Taynuilt
Z Ballachulish is the station for Glencoe and Kinlochleven
② Second class only

Above *Less than two years before closure, the Scottish Region timetable listed four return journeys a day on the Ballachulish branch. Of these, three originated in Oban and involved a reversal at Connel Ferry station. Barcaldine Halt, still open at this date, is only worthy of a mention in the footnotes. In addition to the subsequent loss of the scenic Ballachulish branch, modern rail travellers have also lost the daily (except Sundays) sleeping car coaches from London Euston.*

Below *Coal wagons wait to be unloaded at Creagan station's island platform on 19 April 1952. In the centre you can clearly see the railings around the subway exit from the platform. The station buildings and platform have been sympathetically restored in recent years.*

Right *The trackbed of the railway is clearly visible between Creagan and Appin as it follows the low-lying and fertile Strath Appin. It was but a 2-mile walk from Appin station to Port Appin where foot passengers can still catch the small ferry to the island of Lismore.*

Above *An Easter 1966 view, only two weeks after closure, of the delightfully located Kentallen station, overlooking Loch Linnhe with the mountains of Morvern beyond. In its latter years Kentallen was served by just four trains a day in each direction. The station has since been converted into a hotel with holiday homes built in its grounds. A passenger ferry service to Fort William once operated from the small pier alongside the station.*

Left *North of Appin the trackbed hugs the eastern shore of Loch Linnhe where there are fine views of privately owned Shuna Island and the mountains beyond.*

Below *The narrow and winding A828 is particularly treacherous for walkers and cyclists between Kentallen and South Ballachulish. Fortunately the trackbed of the railway has recently been asphalted to form a cycleway and footpath along this section.*

Above *The old railway line made a detour inland at South Ballachulish. Here the asphalted cycleway and footpath from Kentallen passes through a rock cutting lined with colourful foxgloves.*

Below *Ex-Caledonian Railway 0-4-4 tank No. 55196 waits to depart from Ballachulish terminus with the 3.45pm train to Connel Ferry on 19 April 1952. The loco was built at the St Rollox Works in Glasgow in 1909 and withdrawn from Oban shed at the end of 1955.*

Right *This latticework distant semaphore signal now stands guard over a private drive a mile to the west of Ballachulish station.*

Above *The rusting track at Ballachulish terminus awaits the demolition gang at Easter 1966, just two weeks after closure on 28 March. A goods line once linked the railway here to the Ballachulish slate quarries. The station building is now a doctor's surgery.*

Left *Although nominally independent until becoming part of the LMS in 1923, the Callander & Oban Railway was operated by Caledonian Railway from its opening. Here an old CR notice warns trespassers at Ballachulish station in 1952.*

Right *Ex-CR 0-4-4 tank No. 55196 takes on water at Ballachulish in April 1952. The goods yard still appears to have plenty of traffic at this date. Slate from the nearby quarries was the reason for the building of the line.*

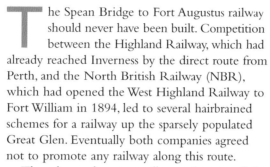
The Spean Bridge to Fort Augustus railway should never have been built. Competition between the Highland Railway, which had already reached Inverness by the direct route from Perth, and the North British Railway (NBR), which had opened the West Highland Railway to Fort William in 1894, led to several hairbrained schemes for a railway up the sparsely populated Great Glen. Eventually both companies agreed not to promote any railway along this route.

The scheme that eventually got the green light was the independent 24-mile Invergarry & Fort Augustus Railway, which was heavily financed by Lord Burton from his brewing empire in Burton-upon-Trent. The brewing connection stuck and the railway was nicknamed 'the beer line'. Built by Formans & McCall, the railway was over-engineered from the start, and the short-lived extension to Fort Augustus Pier at the southerly end of Loch Ness, involving the building of a swing bridge over the Caledonian Canal and a viaduct across the River Oich, was particularly wasteful.

The railway opened on 22 July 1903 and was initially operated by the Highland Railway, which feared that the North British had designs on reaching Inverness along the Great Glen. From the beginning the line was a white elephant and the Highland Railway pulled out in 1907. It was then worked by the North British until 1911 when it, too, withdrew its support and the line ceased to operate. The final twist in this sorry tale came in 1913 when the North British agreed to buy the railway for a tiny fraction of its original cost. At its height there were between four or five passenger trains a day but goods traffic was light and was often conveyed with passenger trains. The summer traffic to Fort Augustus Pier where passengers could enjoy a cruise on Loch Ness never lived up to expectations and the heavily engineered extension was closed within a few years of opening. Under the ownership of the London and North Eastern Railway (LNER), passenger trains were withdrawn in 1933 and the only traffic left was a weekly coal train. Despite an upsurge of traffic during World War II, the line closed completely at the end of 1946.

Left Close to the swing bridge over the Caledonian Canal the route of the Fort Augustus line can be easily identified at Aberchalder by this stone cattle creep and embankment. (See also page 42.)

Above The former junction for the Fort Augustus line, Spean Bridge station on the West Highland line is still open for traffic between Glasgow and Fort William. The station building is now a restaurant.

Left *Seen here in 1914, shortly after being reopened by the NBR, Gairlochy station represents the over-ambitions of the original backers of this line. The grandiose island platform building and sidings set in this remote and sparsely populated part of the Great Glen never lived up to expectations.*

Below *The trackbed of the railway wends its way high above the valley of the River Spean near Gairlochy.*

Above *The bridge abutments of the passenger access bridge at Gairlochy now stand at the entrance to a caravan park. A retaining wall next to the former cattle sidings can be seen in the distance.*

THE LINE TODAY

Spean Bridge station is still open and is served by trains between Glasgow Queen Street and Fort William. Much of the route of the line to Fort Augustus can be followed today along the A82 but care must be taken as many drivers of cars, and particularly motorcycles, on this road tend to use it as a Grand Prix circuit. That apart, there is still much of the railway to be seen.

The first station out of Spean Bridge was Gairlochy (now reached along the B8004). A fairly substantial station with an island platform, and cattle loading sidings, the site is now a caravan park but there are clues to its past everywhere. The trackbed then disappears off onto private land before emerging by the A82 at Glenfintaig Lodge. A well-preserved railway overbridge near the site of Invergloy Platform is another strong railway clue as the trackbed closely follows the route of General Wade's Military Road on the eastern side of Loch Lochy. The site of Invergarry station, 15 miles from Spean Bridge and close to the Laggan swing bridge on the Caledonian Canal, is now a Forestry Commission car park. However, there is still much to see in the undergrowth including the platform edge and fencing across a small bridge parapet. The trackbed of the line along the eastern banks of Loch Oich from here to Aberchalder is now an official cycleway and footpath known as the 'Great Glen Way'. A small stone cattle creep and railway embankment are clearly visible at Aberchalder, close to the famous Bridge of Oich. From here to Fort Augustus the route of the line (and General Wade's Military Road) closely follows the A82.

In Fort Augustus itself, now a popular tourist destination, the old station site is now a school, though the little-used swing bridge over the Caledonian Canal is gone. However, three tall stone piers of the viaduct over the River Oich on the short-lived pier extension still stand testimony to the folly of this line. A stone cutting leads down to the site of the old pier at the southern end of Loch Ness.

Right *North British superpower – a one-coach train headed by a Class 'J37' 0-6-0 No. 9098 halts at Gairlochy station in 1931. There seem to be more staff than passengers! The amount of traffic carried on the line was negligible and passenger trains were withdrawn in 1933.*

Below *A cattle creep and railway embankment in the grounds of Glenfintaig House, between Gairlochy and Invergloy, clearly illustrate the remote location of the line up the Great Glen.*

Right *Invergloy Platform in 1914 shortly after the line was reopened by the NBR. Little used, the spartan tin-roofed waiting room and platform was a request stop for the inhabitants and employees of nearby Invergloy House.*

Below *This well-preserved concrete and girder overbridge stands close to the busy A82, once the route of General Wade's Military Road, near the site of Invergloy Platform.*

Above *Just visible from the A82 far below, this viaduct (seen here in August 1966) between Invergloy and Invergarry demonstrates the over-engineered structures on the railway that were built to accommodate double track. The dream of extending the line right up the Great Glen to Inverness never materialised.*

Right *Located at the southern end of Loch Oich, Invergarry station was a substantial building with an island platform and sidings. The platform was reached via a subway through an archway under these railings. Now used by cyclists and walkers, the trackbed continues as the Great Glen Way along the eastern shore of Loch Oich to Aberchalder.*

Above *Seen here in 1914, the island platform structure at Invergarry was an impressive affair and looks spick and span after the line's reopening by the NBR the previous year.*

Right *Invergarry station returns to nature. More than 60 years since closure the platform edge at Invergarry is still visible through the dense vegetation.*

Above *The timber station building at Aberchalder on the former Fort Augustus branch was still in situ in 1971. It has now been replaced by a modern timber dwelling built on the surviving old platform.*

Left *A cattle creep and embankment near Aberchalder. Beyond is the swing bridge over the Caledonian Canal and the Bridge of Oich – this graceful cantilever bridge was used by road traffic until 1932 when it was replaced by a modern structure and swing bridge.*

FORT-AUGUSTUS and SPEAN BRIDGE.—North British.											
Week Days only.							**Week Days only.**				
Miles		mrn	E	d	s d	s	E				
Fort-Augustus......dep.	8 35	2 52	5 45	30	7 0	.....	.....	...
3½ Aberchalder.............	8 44	2 17	3 6	5 39	.....	.....	...
8 Invergarry.............	8 54	2 31	3 20	5 50	7 17	.....	...
15½ Invergloy Platform......	a	a	a	a	a	.....	...
20¾ Gairlochy.................	9 18	3 18	4 7	6 18	7 39	.....	...
23 Spean Bridge 775 ...arr.	9 25	3 30	4 19	6 26	7 47	.....	...

Miles			mrn	h	d s	E				
Spean Bridge ......dep.	10 53	5 56	9 8	0	.....	...
2½ Gairlochy	10 34	7 6	17	8 8	.....	...
7½ Invergloy Platform.....	a	a	a	.....	...
15 Invergarry............	10 37	4 45	6 41	8 31	.....	...
19½ Aberchalder.............	10 47	4 58	6 51	.....	...
23 Fort-Augustus......arr.	10 55	5 10	6 59	8 49	.....	...

a Stop when required.   **d** Through Trains to and from Fort William, see page 727.
h Through Train from Fort William on Saturdays, see page 727.   **E** Except Saturdays.

Left *One year before the NBR became part of the LNER in the 1923 Grouping, most passenger trains on the Fort Augustus line took a leisurely 50 minutes to cover 23 miles. The branch engine started and ended its day's work at Fort Augustus where it spent each night in the small engine shed.*

Left and below *LNER days at Fort Augustus station on 23 July 1931. Ex-NBR 4-4-2 tank No. 9155 waits to depart with the 4.30pm one-coach train to Fort William. The signal guarding the pier extension line can be seen on the far left of the lower photograph.*

Left *A substantial viaduct was built at great expense over the River Oich to carry trains the short distance from Fort Augustus station down to a pier at the southern end of Loch Ness. Passenger trains were withdrawn on this section in 1905 and goods trains ceased in 1924.*

Below *With their castellated turrets, the three stone piers of the viaduct over the River Oich stand testimony to the great financial losses suffered by the railway's backers.*

Above *A deep rock cutting and ledge was excavated to carry the railway down to a pier on the shore of Loch Ness at Fort Augustus. Rarely used, by 23 July 1931, when this photograph was taken, the track was already being taken over by nature.*

Below *The end of the line at Fort Augustus station on 16 June 1927 from the site of the swing bridge across the Caledonian Canal. The construction costs of the heavily engineered mile-long extension to the pier financially crippled the railway. It was rarely used and soon fell into disuse.*

MUIR OF ORD TO FORTROSE

The Black Isle is a low-lying peninsula that sits between the Beauly and Cromarty Firths north of Inverness. Although endowed with fertile farmland and a healthy coastal fishing industry the isle was isolated from the new railway that opened between Inverness and Dingwall in 1862. The nearest station to the isle on that line was at Muir of Ord and, in 1890, the necessary parliamentary powers were obtained for a 15¾-mile branch line to Rosemarkie. In the event this lightly engineered line across undulating farmland was completed only as far as Fortrose, to which it opened for traffic on 1 February 1894.

Relying mainly on agricultural and fish traffic the 13½-mile rural branch line saw only a basic three return passenger trains each weekday – as with most of the railways in rural Scotland there were no trains on the Sabbath.

Passenger services were withdrawn on 1 October 1951 but the weekly goods trains continued until complete closure on 13 June 1960.

THE LINE TODAY

Although Muir of Ord station is still open on the Inverness to Dingwall line little remains of the lightly engineered branch line to Fortrose. To the east of Muir of Ord much of the trackbed beyond Muir of Tarradale is now a farm track and footpath. Several old railway bridges and cattle creeps along here remain intact. Further east the wooden structure of Redcastle station has been well restored as a private residence. Both the stations at Allangrange and Munlochy have been demolished but a section of railway embankment with stone cattle creeps can be seen alongside the A832 east of Munlochy. Here there is a small car park and bird hide overlooking the wetlands of Munlochy Bay. The site of Avoch station is now a housing estate while the station yard at Fortrose is now a car park. The only clue to the former railway here is a small brick-built and creeper-clad office and weighbridge that once served the goods yard. In less than 50 years the Fortrose branch has more or less disappeared.

Left *Just over a mile to the east of Muir of Ord the trackbed at Muir of Tarradale is now a peaceful public footpath. In the opposite direction a farm track runs along the route of the railway towards Redcastle.*

Above *Ex-Highland Railway 'L' Class 4-4-0 No. 14277 on the turntable at Muir of Ord on 21 May 1928. Known as 'Skye Bogies', nine of these locos were built at Lochgorm Works, Inverness, between 1882 and 1901.*

Above *Ex-Highland Railway 'Ben' Class 4-4-0 No. 14406 'Ben Slioch' backs on to the 3.35pm one-coach train to Fortrose at Muir of Ord on 10 April 1946. This loco was one of a batch of nine built at Lochgorm Works between 1899 and 1900. One member of this class, BR No. 54398 'Ben Alder', was scheduled for preservation but, mysteriously, was cut-up after years in storage.*

Right *This stone bridge over a farm track at Muir of Tarradale is one of the few structures on the Fortrose branch that still remains today.*

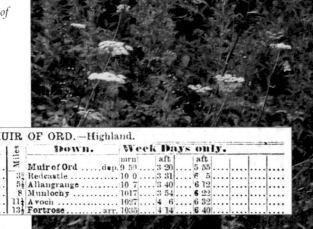

FORTROSE and MUIR OF ORD.—Highland.

Miles	Up.	Week Days only.						Miles	Down.	Week Days only.					
		mrn	aft	aft						mrn	aft	aft			
	Fortrose.......dep.	8 30	1245	4 40					Muir of Ord ......dep.	9 50	3 20	5 55			
2¼	Avoch	8 40	1255	4 50				3¾	Redcastle	10 0	3 31	6 5			
5¼	Munlochy............	8 55	1 10	5 5				5¼	Allangrange	10 7	3 40	6 12			
8	Allangrange........	9 6	1 21	5 16				8	Munlochy	1017	3 54	6 22			
9¾	Redcastle...........	9 20	1 35	5 36				11¼	Avoch	1027	4 6	6 32			
13½	Muir of Ord 870 arr	9 30	1 45	5 40				13½	Fortrose ....arr.	1035	4 14	6 40			

Above *The Highland Railway passenger timetable for 1922 shows three return journeys on weekdays over the Fortrose branch. The leisurely journey along the 13½-mile branch could take up to an hour – presumably to allow shunting of goods wagons at intermediate stations.*

Above *A few locals come out to witness the passage of the last train at a farm crossing near Avoch on 14 June 1960. The line had closed officially the previous day but an enthusiasts special, headed by ex-Caledonian Railway 0-6-0 No. 57594, carried out the last rites.*

Below *The first stop out of Muir of Ord, Redcastle station, has been restored as a private residence. It is the only station building on the Fortrose branch that remains intact today.*

Right *With no major engineering features, the Fortrose branch crossed the rolling farmland of the Black Isle. The trackbed is still visible alongside the A832 just to the east of Munlochy.*

Above *The final train on the Fortrose branch pauses at Munlochy on 14 June 1960. A group of enthusiasts and mourners wander round the station paying their last respects. The building has since been demolished and the site is now a children's playground.*

Below *Continuing its slow journey to Fortrose on the branch line's last day, veteran ex-Caledonian Railway 0-6-0 No. 57594 pauses at Avoch station. Passenger services had ceased here 10 years earlier. The building was eventually demolished and the site is now a housing estate.*

Above *A last look at Fortrose station on the line's final day, 14 June 1960. Of interest is the two-tone Sunbeam Rapier (a classic product of the Rootes Group) and a sit-up-and-beg Ford Popular. Happy days! The former station site is now a car park.*

Left *Located on the site of the former railway yard, this weighbridge and creeper-clad office is now the only reminder of the old railway at Fortrose.*

Above *Happier days at Fortrose before the withdrawal of passenger services. Ex-Highland Railway 'Ben Class' 4-4-0 No. 14406 'Ben Slioch' is manually turned at Fortrose after hauling the 3.35pm train from Muir of Ord on 10 April 1946.*

Left *No. 57594 has just been turned at Fortrose on 14 June 1960 before departing to Muir of Ord with the very last train on the branch. The enthusiasts special is made up of a varied selection of both old and new rolling stock. The loco, already 60 years old when photographed here, went on to survive for another 2½ years before withdrawal from Inverness engine shed at the end of 1962.*

53

BOAT OF GARTEN TO KEITH

The Great North of Scotland Railway (GNoSR) had reached Keith from Aberdeen in 1856. A year later the Keith & Dufftown Railway obtained parliamentary powers to build a railway connecting the two towns.

Construction was slow due to financial difficulties but the line eventually opened on 21 February 1862. The railway was soon in deeper financial trouble and was required to seek help from the GNoSR, which took it over in 1866.

The Strathspey Railway was incorporated in 1861 to extend the Keith & Dufftown line from Dufftown to Abernethy (now Nethy Bridge). It opened on 1 July 1863. Worked from the onset by the GNoSR, the railway suffered due to the lack of a connection with the Inverness and Perth Junction Railway (soon to be the Highland Railway) which opened from Aviemore to Forres via Boat of Garten in September of that year. A connection was built to the north of Boat of Garten in 1865 but prolonged wranglings over the cost of signalling at the junction led to a three-year delay before Strathspey trains could enter Boat of Garten station along their own dedicated track.

Closely following the valley of the River Spey, the building of the Strathspey Railway involved major engineering features including deep cuttings and numerous bridges over the meandering river. Trains from Boat of Garten, usually three return journeys a day, connected with trains from Keith to Elgin at Craigellachie. Traffic was light in this sparsely populated region although the many whisky distilleries on this line soon became connected by rail with two – Cromdale and Dailuaine – having their own short branch lines. Tourism was slow to take off but by the early 20th century the scenic delights of the Strathspey line were being marketed, leading to the running of excursion trains in the summer.

Goods traffic saw an increase during World War II following the increase in demand for timber grown in the surrounding forests.

Above *A Class 'K2' 2-6-0 loco takes on water at Boat of Garten engine shed on 10 August 1956 prior to working a goods train. Also in view is ex-Highland Railway 4-4-0 No. 54398 'Ben Alder' which was kept here pending restoration and had at this stage been moved out of the shed because of the unsafe roof. The engine was scrapped some years later.*

Left *The bridge over the River Spey at Ballindalloch is one of the highlights on the Speyside Way long-distance path. The bridge was built for the opening of the line by G McFarlane of Dundee in 1863.*

Diesel railbuses were introduced under British Railways in 1958 and four new halts were opened to serve local farms and distilleries along the line. Sadly, none of these improvements could prevent the eventual closure of the line under the notorious 'Beeching axe'.

The first to go were passenger trains on the Speyside line between Boat of Garten and Craigellachie which were withdrawn on 18 October 1965. Goods services, mainly to serve the distilleries, continued between Boat of Garten and Aberlour until 4 November 1968. The Aberlour to Craigellachie section finally closed to goods on 15 November 1971. Meanwhile, passenger trains between Keith Junction and Craigellachie (along with trains to Rothes and Elgin) were withdrawn on 6 May 1968. Goods traffic between Keith Junction and Dufftown ceased on 1 October 1985 although the line was later retained for use by luxury charter passenger trains visiting the Glenfiddich Distillery in what is now termed 'the Whisky Capital of the World'.

THE LINE TODAY

Railway enthusiasts and walkers are fortunate that much of the trackbed and infrastructure of this scenic line is accessible along the Speyside Way long-distance path. One of only four long-distance paths in Scotland, the 65-mile Speyside Way was opened in 2000, and goes from Buckie to Aviemore closely following the course of the River Spey.

Above *Nethy Bridge station, the first stop out of Boat of Garten, on 11 July 1957. Originally the terminus of the line from Craigellachie, the station was called Abernethy until 1867. A small request halt, serving Ballifurth Farm, was opened 2 miles further on in the Grantown direction following the introduction of diesel railbuses in 1958.*

Right *More than 40 years after closure the overgrown platform and derelict station building at Grantown-on-Spey East are still awaiting some tender loving care.*

Before exploring the old line from Boat of Garten to Dufftown you can take a trip on the steam-hauled Strathspey Railway which currently operates a heritage line between Aviemore, Boat of Garten and Broomhill.

Between Boat of Garten and Dufftown the majority of the station buildings and platforms have been beautifully restored. Some are private residences although the station at Ballindalloch is a hostel, Knockando station (renamed Tamdhu) is in the grounds of a distillery and Aberlour station is a tearoom. The old railway bridge over the Spey at Ballindalloch is particularly impressive.

The Keith to Dufftown line was taken over by a group of volunteers and opened as the Keith & Dufftown Railway in 2000. Diesel railcar services operate at weekends from Easter until the end of September between Keith Town station and Dufftown.

Above *Despite the planting of pine trees the platform at Advie station is still clearly visible today. A small request halt serving Dalvey Farm, between Cromdale and Advie, was opened on 15 June 1959.*

Right *Built at the St Rollox Works, Glasgow in 1908 ex-Caledonian Railway 0-6-0 No. 57634 pauses at Advie with a freight train in the 1950s. Diesel locos had taken over from steam by the end of the decade but the 'Caley Goods' lived on until withdrawal from Dalry Road engine shed in August 1963.*

Left *Set in the idyllic Spey Valley, the beautifully restored Cromdale station is now a private residence.*

Left inset *The epitome of a Scottish branch line – ex-CR 0-6-0 No. 57591 halts at Cromdale with a train from Craigellachie to Boat of Garten on 10 August 1956. In an effort to reduce running costs, these vintage trains were made redundant two years later and replaced by four-wheel diesel railbuses.*

Below *G McFarlane of Dundee was obviously very proud of his bridge across the Spey at Ballindalloch when it was opened in 1863.*

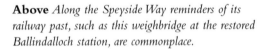

Above *Along the Speyside Way reminders of its railway past, such as this weighbridge at the restored Ballindalloch station, are commonplace.*

Below *The old station building at Ballindalloch is now a hostel. Certain sections of the Speyside Way are also suitable for cyclists and horse riders.*

Above *All is quiet at Ballindalloch station in the early afternoon of 11 April 1946. Today the signal box is gone and the growth of vegetation on the platform makes this view difficult to photograph.*

Right *The steel latticework bridge over the River Spey at Ballindalloch is one of the engineering highlights of the old Speyside railway. Now part of the Speyside Way, a short stroll across the bridge and along the trackbed takes the walker to the beautifully restored Blacksboat station.*

Left inset *A hive of activity at Blacksboat station on 11 April 1946. Passenger traffic was never heavy along this line, which mainly depended on goods traffic to and from the many whisky distilleries that it served.*

Left *Now a private residence, the beautifully restored Blacksboat station is located in an idyllic riverside spot on the route of the Speyside Way.*

Above *The old goods shed at Blacksboat is a major achievement of sympathetic restoration.*

Above *Knockando station building, signal box and double platform have all been sympathetically restored by the nearby whisky distillery as their visitor centre. The station has been renamed 'Tamdhu' in honour of their famous brand of single malt. Served by diesel railbuses introduced on the line in November 1958, two small request halts for distillery workers at Gilbey's Cottages and Imperial Cottages were opened between Knockando and Carron on 15 June 1959. A private halt serving Knockando House was opened in 1869.*

Above *Carron station building, complete with rusty old clock and cast-iron drinking fountain, is now disused and stands close to the famous Imperial Distillery, which opened alongside the railway in 1897. The distillery, which once had its own network of sidings, is now mothballed and awaiting development.*

Left *Side by side, at Balmenach Distillery in October 1966, one mode of transport soon to be extinguished by the other. Balmenach was the most southerly of two Speyside distilleries with its own 'pug' locomotive, in this case shunting inbound barley and outbound spirit over a short private branch line to exchange sidings at Cromdale station. The daily freight train over the Speyside line was withdrawn by British Rail in October 1968 – with traffic then concentrated on modern railheads in Dufftown and Elgin. The Kilmarnock-built 0-4-0 steam locomotive has been preserved on the Strathspey Railway at nearby Boat of Garten.*

Below *The large nameboard dwarfs the basic wooden hut and short platform at Dailuaine Halt. A request stop only, there appears to have been three passengers with a pushchair who have just alighted on 11 July 1957.*

Below *Aberlour station is now a tea room and the old station yard down to the Spey has been beautifully landscaped. The station opened for business in 1863 and was closed to passengers on 18 October 1965. Goods traffic to the distilleries lingered on until November 1971.*

Above *Pickersgill GNoSR Class 'D40' 4-4-0 No. 62265 leaves Craigellachie on a frosty morning with a train to Boat of Garten early in 1952. Only 44 steam locos from the GNoSR survived through to nationalisation in 1948. No. 62265 was built in 1909 and was withdrawn from Keith shed early in 1957. The last GNoSR loco to remain in service, No. 62277 'Gordon Highlander', has since been preserved.*

Top left inset *A young Richard Casserley, the railway photographer, inspects ex-GNoSR Class 'D40' 4-4-0 No. 6915 of Keith shed after arrival at Craigellachie with the 12.55pm train from Boat of Garten on 11 April 1946.*

Left *Today the site of Craigellachie station is now a car park for users of the Speyside Way.*

Left inset *Passengers wait for an Elgin to Keith train at Craigellachie on 11 April 1946. The Strathspey line platforms are out of sight on the left. Beyond the station is the now demolished bridge over the Spey.*

Above *Rush hour at Craigellachie on 11 July 1957. BR Standard Class 2 2-6-0 No. 78054 has just arrived from Boat of Garten with a track recording coach. Just over a year later steam-hauled passenger trains were replaced by four-wheel diesel railbuses. No. 78054 was only 18 months old when seen here and was withdrawn at the end of 1965.*

Below *Saved from closure by volunteers in 2000, the 11-mile Keith & Dufftown Railway operates a diesel service from Dufftown to Keith Town on weekends between Easter and the end of September.*

Left *A few passengers wait for a train at Keith Town in the 1930s. Until the late 20th century the Dufftown line continued to Keith Junction where it met the Inverness to Aberdeen main line. Sadly that short connection is now severed and the Keith & Dufftown Railway is no longer connected to the national rail network.*

Below *This superb reconstruction of the original GNoSR split-level station building at Keith Town was completed in 2003. Compare it to the photograph on the left. The distant signal marks the end of the line at Keith.*

Above *Still served by regular interval trains on the Inverness to Aberdeen main line, Keith Junction station still boasts sidings and an old GNoSR goods shed that are now used by Network Rail maintenance crews.*

Below *Keith engine shed supplied motive power for trains to Dufftown and Speyside. This view of the shed taken in 1949, a year after nationalisation, shows two of the GNoSR 'D40' 4-4-0s plus an ex-Great Eastern Railway 'B12' 4-6-0 and a fairly new Thompson 'B1' 4-6-0. 'Dieselisation' of ex-GNoSR lines was complete by 1960 and the shed closed to steam in January 1961. It was subsequently used as a diesel depot until it was demolished in 1976.*

ELGIN TO TILLYNAUGHT AND BANFF

The history of the railway along the Morayshire coast is a complex and convoluted tale. By the 1850s Britain was in the grip of a severe depression and, following the completion of the Aberdeen to Keith line in 1856, the Great North of Scotland Railway (GNoSR) was in no financial state to build new railways. However, an independent company, the Banff, Portsoy and Strathisla Railway (BP&SR), received parliamentary consent in 1857 to build a line from Grange, on the GNoSR main line from Aberdeen, to Banff with a branch from Tillynaught to Portsoy. The line opened in July 1859.

Unfortunately the BP&SR was never a financial success and the GNoSR took over the running of the railway in 1863, renaming it the Banffshire Railway. The latter company also fell on hard times and was taken over again by the GNoSR in 1867. It was not until 1882 that parliamentary consent was given to extend the railway along the coast from Portsoy to Elgin. The new extension opened in stages – Portsoy to Tochieneal in April 1884; Elgin to Garmouth in August; and Tochieneal to Garmouth in May 1886 – and involved the building of high embankments and viaducts around Cullen and a long bridge over the Spey near Garmouth.

With the opening of the Morayshire coastal line the GNoSR now had two routes between Aberdeen and Elgin (the Elgin to Keith 'direct' line had been opened by its competitor, the Highland Railway, in 1858): via a new junction at Cairnie, south of Grange, and along the coastal line, a distance of 87 miles; and via Keith and Craigellachie, a distance of nearly 81 miles.

However, the Aberdeen to Inverness service via the 'direct route' was subject to years of quarrelling and feuding between the Highland Railway and the GNoSR – a situation that was only put right in 1897 by the arbitration of the

Railway & Canal Commissioners. The two circuitous GNoSR routes from Aberdeen to Elgin soon became secondary lines and were subsequently only served by stopping trains until their closure in the 1960s.

In 1923 the GNoSR became part of the newly formed London & North Eastern Railway and the coastal line settled down to a timetable of six trains each way on weekdays (no trains on Sundays), including one that had through-coaches between Elgin and Aberdeen. Fish traffic was

Above *The final departure board at Elgin (East) station on Saturday 4 May 1968 prior to the last train departing for Aberdeen via Buckie. Also posted is the last train from Elgin to Aberdeen via Craigellachie and Dufftown. Apart from the Aberdeen to Inverness service all of the destinations once served by trains from Elgin are no longer rail connected.*

Left *This attractive latticework pedestrian bridge still stands over the trackbed of the line at Buckie. Thanks to Dr Beeching, the rail journey along this attractive stretch of coastline is now denied to us.*

Table 36 — ABERDEEN, ELGIN and INVERNESS — Week Days only

Left *Between Elgin and Garmouth much of the trackbed has been swallowed up by farmland. With its adjoining embankments flattened, this stone railway bridge near Urquhart is now totally stranded in the midst of Morayshire farmland.*

Above *Seen here at Garmouth, the trackbed is now a dedicated footpath and part of the National Cycle Network Route 1. Highlights on this coastal section include the massive steel structure of nearby Spey Bridge.*

heavy, especially from the port of Buckie which had one of the largest drifter fleets in Scotland. The Banff branch had a fairly respectable service that connected with the coastal line trains at Tillynaught Junction.

Under British Railways the GNoSR lines north of Aberdeen saw the early introduction of diesels but despite these and other cost-saving measures the Morayshire coastal route and the Banff branch soon became victims of 'the Beeching axe'. First to go were passenger services on the Tillynaught to Banff branch, which were withdrawn on 6 July 1964. Goods traffic on this line and both passenger and goods on the coastal line between Cairnie Junction and Elgin were withdrawn on 6 May 1968.

THE LINE TODAY

Elgin railway station is still open and is served by trains between Aberdeen and Inverness. More than 40 years after closure much of the route of

the Morayshire coastal line and the Banff branch can easily be followed by using Ordnance Survey Landranger Maps Nos. 28 and 29. Between Elgin and Garmouth much of the trackbed has disappeared beneath farmland but isolated railway bridges, such as that near Urquhart, can be spotted stranded in the middle of fields.

On the most scenic part of the line, between Garmouth and Cullen, the trackbed is now a cycleway and footpath and takes in the mighty Spey Bridge and the magnificent viaducts at Cullen. Seaviews abound, especially on the coast-hugging section east of Portgordon. Some sections of the trackbed are also now designated as part of the National Cycle Network Route 1.

From Banff it is but a short walk over the bridge across the River Deveron to the small but busy port and shipbuilding town of Macduff, once the terminus of the 30-mile long GNoSR branch from Inveramsay.

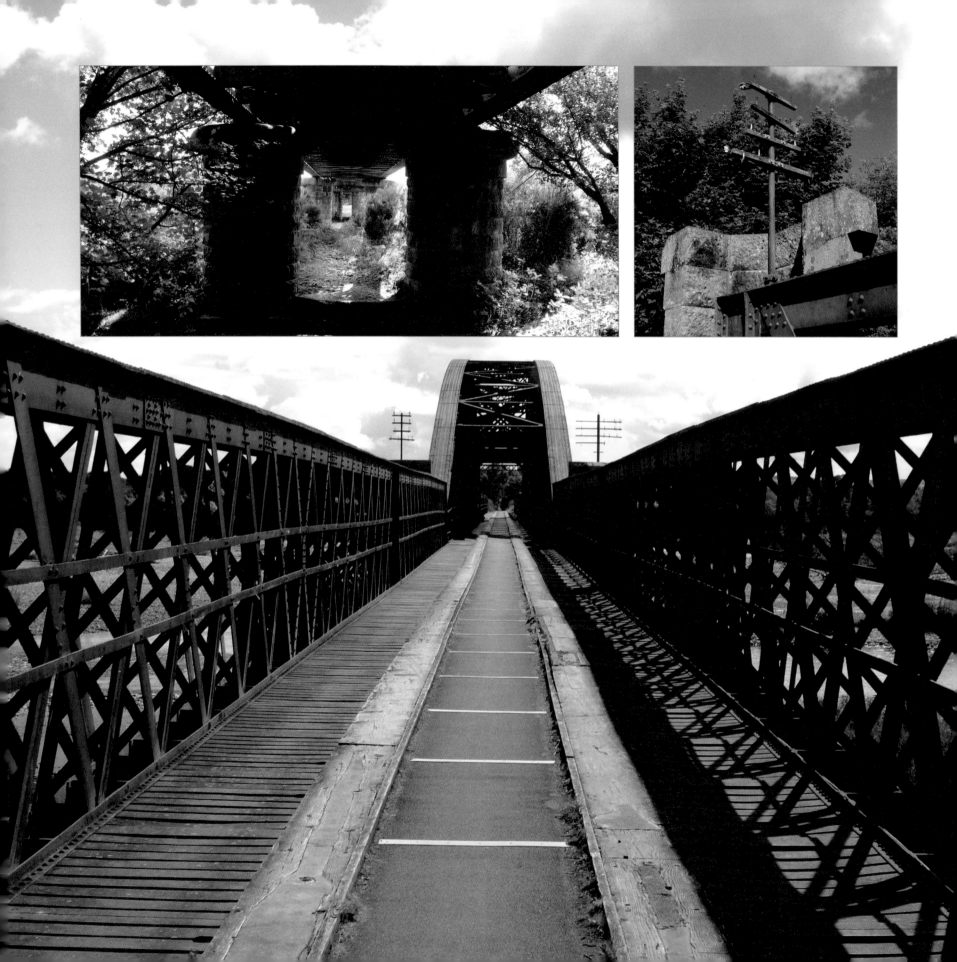

Left *One of the engineering highlights on the line is the massive single-track bridge across the River Spey near Garmouth. On the far side is Spey Bay, once a major salmon fishing centre. Both the Speyside Way long-distance path and Route 1 of the National Cycle Network now cross this bridge. The old telegraph post has somehow survived since closure of the line in 1968.*

Right *Eastwards from Spey Bay the line crossed this stretch of low-lying farmland before reaching the coast at Portgordon.*

Below *Glorious seaviews were once enjoyed by passengers along this stretch of coastal railway at Portgordon. Now the trackbed is enjoyed by walkers and cyclists.*

Above *'The 'Beeching axe' finally falls on the Morayshire coastal line – this sad scene had already occurred at hundreds of stations across Britain. Another local railway that closed to passengers on 6 May 1968 was the line from Keith Junction to Elgin via Dufftown and Craigellachie.*

Above *Just weeks before the complete closure of the Moray coastal line on 6 May 1968, Birmingham Railway Carriage & Wagon Company Type 2 diesel D5335 shunts coal wagons in Buckie goods yard. A bout of feverish activity followed its arrival as the coal was weighed, bagged and then loaded aboard lorries for local distribution.*

Below *Still used by pedestrians this attractive Victorian latticework footbridge over the trackbed at Buckie seems to have taken on a more exciting role for the local children. The blue sea of Spey Bay is but a short distance away.*

Left *Along with Spey Bridge, the two viaducts at Cullen are the engineering highlights of the Morayshire coastal line. From the top of this viaduct, accessible for walkers and cyclists, there are panoramic views of the fishing village – famous for the smoked haddock soup known as Cullen Skink.*

Right *This piece of modern sculpture marks the passage of the National Cycle Network Route 1 on the railway embankment close to Cullen Viaduct.*

Above *The A98 passes under one of the arches of this old railway viaduct in the centre of picturesque Cullen.*

Above *A North British Locomotive Co. Type 2 (Class 21) diesel rumbles off Cullen Viaduct with an eastbound freight in September 1961. Introduced in 1959 these were one of the most unreliable classes of diesels ordered by British Rail and had been withdrawn by 1968. Twenty had been fitted with uprated engines between 1963 and 1965 and reclassified as Class 29 but even these had gone to the scrapheap by 1971.*

Above *A full head of steam at Tillynaught on 9 July 1957. Ex-LNER 'B1' 4-6-0 No. 61242 enters from the north with the 6.15pm Elgin to Aberdeen. On the left BR Standard Class 4 2-6-4 tank No. 80122 waits patiently with the 6.50pm Keith to Elgin; on the right ex-Caledonian Railway 0-4-4 tank No. 55185 waits to head off down the branch line with the 7.35pm to Banff.*

Above *Birmingham Railway Carriage and Wagon Company Type 2 D5331 waits to depart from Tillynaught Junction with the final train from Elgin to Aberdeen via Buckie on 4 May 1968.*

Right *Tucked away behind seafront cottages the branch line into Banff at Scotstown is now a public footpath. In its last year of operation the branch was still well served by 10 return journeys each weekday.*

Table 39

TILLYNAUGHT and BANFF

Miles		am	am 7C 5	am	am 1015		pm		pm		Week Days only				pm 3C55		pm 6 20
	Aberdeen .... dep			8 56			1155	5	3		2 10			4 50	5 55		
1½	Tillynaught .... dep	7 15			1021		12½	1 15				3 5		4 56			8 21
3	Ordens Halt																
4¼	Ladysbridge																
5¼	Bridgefoot Halt																
6	Golf Club House Halt				1030		1210		1 25			3 15			6 10		8 30
	Banff .... arr	7 35	9 16														

Miles		am	am	am	am				pm		Week Days only			pm		pm 7 50
	Banff .... dep	6 45	8 30	9 50	1120		1230	2 30		23			4 40		5 25	
¾	Golf Club House Halt dep															
1¾	Bridgefoot Halt				1136	1246		2 37								
2¾	Ladysbridge	6 52	8 37	9 57											5 25	
4½	Ordens Halt															
6	Tillynaught	7	8 45	10 5	1145	1255		2 45		3 38			4 32		5 40	8 5
	Aberdeen .... arr	9 4		1150				4 38					6849			9 48

B Change at Cairnie Junction.
C Change at Cairnie Junction. On Saturdays arrives Aberdeen 6 51 pm
xx All trains call to set down on request to guard or when there are passengers to take up

Above *Still in its LNER livery and carrying its pre-nationalisation number of 2256, ex-GNoSR 4-4-0 No. 2256 stands under the single-road station shed at Banff after arriving with the 10.35am train from Tillynaught on 16 June 1949.*

Above *Approaching journey's end at Banff. The final approaches to the station offered passengers tantalising glimpses of Boyndie Bay across the rooftops.*

Left *Ex-Caledonian Railway 0-4-4 tank No. 55185 gets ready for its next turn of duty at Banff engine shed on 9 July 1957. Built at the St Rollox Works in 1907, this loco was withdrawn from Keith engine shed in 1961.*

INVERAMSAY TO MACDUFF

The first railway built by the Great North of Scotland Railway (GNoSR), between Kittybrewster and Huntly, opened to traffic in 1854. By this time there had already been a proposal to build a railway from Inverurie to Macduff via Old Meldrum. However, nothing came of this and in 1855 the Banff, Macduff & Turriff Junction Railway received parliamentary consent to build a railway from Inveramsay, where there was to be a junction with the GNoSR main line, as far as Turriff. The GNoSR became a shareholder and agreed to operate the line. With no major engineering features the 18-mile line was opened on 5 September 1857.

In the meantime another railway company, the Banff, Macduff & Turriff Extension Railway, had obtained parliamentary consent to complete the railway northwards from Turriff to Macduff. Again

the GNoSR became a shareholder and undertook to operate the line which opened to a temporary terminus some distance from the town of Macduff on 4 June 1860. Neither of these railway companies were a financial success and they were absorbed into the GNoSR in 1866. The long-awaited extension of the railway to a more convenient terminus high above Macduff was opened in 1872. Traffic was never heavy on this rural line and the lack of a rail connection to the harbour at Macduff certainly did not help matters.

By 1922, just one year before the GNoSR became part of the newly formed London & North Eastern Railway, there were five return passenger trains along the branch each weekday. Branch locomotives started and ended their day at Macduff and spent each night in the town's small

Left *This fine stone arched bridge once carried the Macduff line over the meandering River Urie near Pitcaple. Trains on the nearby Aberdeen to Inverness line still operate today.*

Above *An enthusiasts special, headed by ex-GNoSR 'D40' 4-4-0 No. 49 'Gordon Highlander', visited the Macduff branch on 13 June 1960. Here the train halts at Rothienorman which closed to passengers in 1951.*

Left *The old station site and buildings at Fyvie are now an agricultural merchant's yard. Goods trains continued to call here until complete closure of the line in 1966.*

Above *North of Fyvie this rusting railway bridge over the Howe of Auchterless stands next to the A947. Meandering through lightly populated Aberdeenshire farmland the railway was never an economic success.*

two-road engine shed. The decline in local traffic after World War II, escalating operational costs and increasing road competition, led to the withdrawal of passenger services on the line as early as 1 October 1951. Freight trains continued to operate but even these were withdrawn between Turriff and Macduff in August 1961. Freight traffic over the southern end of the line from Inveramsay to Turriff soldiered on until 3 January 1966 when the line was completely closed.

THE LINE TODAY

Inveramsay station on the Aberdeen to Inverness line is no longer open. The nearest station is Inverurie, about 3 miles to the southeast. Much of this line passes through agricultural land and many parts of it have long since disappeared. However, on closer observation many bridges, cuttings and some station sites can still be discovered. The route of the line can be followed by using Ordnance Survey Landranger Maps Nos. 29 and 38.

The first sighting of the railway, a splendid stone arched bridge over the River Urie, can be seen to the north of the notorious A96 near Pitcaple. Wartle station is now a private residence, and the station at Rothienorman has long since disappeared. The station yard at Fyvie is now an agricultural merchant's yard and Auchterless station building is a private residence. Turriff station yard is a caravan site where a number of loading platforms are still extant.

The trackbed north of Turriff is now a footpath to just beyond Tillyfar where the old level crossing posts can still be seen. The route north of King Edward closely follows the A947 to the outskirts of Macduff. Here the road drops down past the distillery to sea level while the trackbed of the old line remains at a higher level, closely following the contours of the Hill of Doune until it reaches the site of the old terminus high above the town. Although now an industrial yard both the engine shed and terminus building still survive, albeit with many modifications for their modern-day uses.

Above *No. 49 'Gordon Highlander' halts at Turriff station with an enthusiasts special on 13 June 1960. The train was made up of an interesting selection of British Rail, ex-LNER and preserved carriages. The station yard at Turriff is now a caravan park. Although some of the loading platforms still exist the wooden station buildings and footbridge have long since disappeared.*

Above *The unusually sited signal box at Turriff, seen here in June 1960, was reached via a ramp from the platform.*

Right *The trackbed of the line north of Turriff to beyond Tillyfar is now a public footpath. Beyond here Plaidy station has long ago disappeared.*

Right inset *The only preserved locomotive of the Great North of Scotland Railway, No. 49 'Gordon Highlander', heads the enthusiasts special that traversed the Macduff line on 13 June 1960. It is seen here at King Edward where the single covered wagon on the left is an indicator of the amount of goods traffic in the year before complete closure.*

Above *On the approach to Macduff, the railway winds around the contours of the Hill of Doune. With its girder bridge long gone, the stone abutments have been bricked up to prevent access.*

Left *High above the harbour, Macduff station was not conveniently sited for the town it served. Here, on 16 June 1949, ex-GNoSR 4-4-0 'D40' No. 62279 'Glen Grant' stands at the single platform with the 12.30pm to Inveramsay. The roof of the engine shed is just visible in the left foreground.*

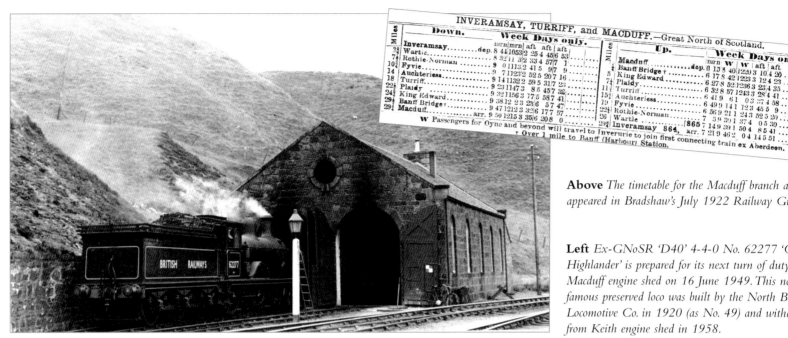

INVERAMSAY, TURRIFF, and MACDUFF.—Great North of Scotland.

	Down.	Week Days only.		Up.	Week Days only.

(Bradshaw timetable for the Macduff branch, July 1922)

Above *The timetable for the Macduff branch as it appeared in Bradshaw's July 1922 Railway Guide.*

Left *Ex-GNoSR 'D40' 4-4-0 No. 62277 'Gordon Highlander' is prepared for its next turn of duty at Macduff engine shed on 16 June 1949. This now famous preserved loco was built by the North British Locomotive Co. in 1920 (as No. 49) and withdrawn from Keith engine shed in 1958.*

Right *No. 62279 'Glen Grant' waits to depart from the tiny station at Macduff with a train for Inveramsay in June 1949. This loco was built by the North British Locomotive Co. in 1920 and withdrawn from Kittybrewster engine shed in 1955. The line to Inveramsay closed to passengers in October 1951.*

Left *Probably the last passenger train to visit the goods-only station at Macduff was run on 13 June 1960. Viewed from inside the small station shed, preserved ex-GNoSR 'D40' 4-4-0 No. 62277 'Gordon Highlander' tops up its water after being turned on the turntable before returning down the branch to Inveramsay. Goods traffic between Macduff and Turriff was withdrawn the following year.*

KINNABER JUNCTION TO STANLEY JUNCTION
VIA FORFAR

The history of the Caledonian Railway's route from Perth to Aberdeen is, like much of Scotland's railway history, a complicated tale of the aspirations of independent railway companies during the years of 'Railway Mania'.

First on the scene was the quaint Arbroath & Forfar Railway, which was built to a gauge of 5ft 6in and opened in 1839. The section of this line between Guthrie and Forfar eventually became part of the Caledonian's vital route between Perth and Aberdeen. The railway was converted to standard gauge in 1847 and leased to the Aberdeen Railway in 1848.

The second of these companies was the Scottish Midland Junction Railway which received parliamentary consent to build a line between Perth and Forfar in 1845. This opened in 1848. Branches from Coupar Angus to Blairgowrie and from Kirriemuir Junction to Kirriemuir were opened in 1855 and at the end of 1854 respectively.

The third company that completed the link between Guthrie and Aberdeen via Bridge of Dun was the Aberdeen Railway, which was incorporated in 1845. The line, which included a branch to Brechin, opened in stages and by 1850 had reached Aberdeen Ferryhill. By 1848 it had leased the Arbroath & Forfar Railway, and in 1856 it merged with the Scottish Midland Junction Railway. This whole undertaking was then absorbed by the Caledonian Railway (CR) in 1866.

There was now set in place a major railway line linking Aberdeen to Glasgow via Perth along Caledonian Railway tracks. At Kinnaber Junction, just north of Montrose, the CR met the North British Railway. The junction was the 'finishing

Left *A mile southwest from Bridge of Dun the railway once crossed this bridge over the River South Esk. A popular spot with fishermen, the river bank here is also a perfect location for a picnic. The line between Bridge of Dun and Forfar closed to all traffic on 4 September 1967 leaving only the truncated eastern and western sections open for goods until the early 1980s.*

Above *The Gresley 'A4' Pacifics performed their swan song on the Aberdeen to Glasgow three-hour expresses in the early 1960s. Here, No. 60009 'Union of South Africa' approaches Bridge of Dun with an up express on 5 May 1965. Built at Doncaster in 1937 this fine loco was withdrawn from Aberdeen Ferryhill engine shed in June 1966. It has since been preserved.*

Above *An ex-Caledonian Railway 0-6-0 runs round its train at Bridge of Dun on 17 June 1962 after hauling an enthusiasts special up the goods-only Brechin branch. The scene is much the same today although the double footbridge has since been dismantled.*

post' for trains from the south during the famous 'Race to the North' in 1888 and 1895 between competing trains on the West Coast and East Coast Main Lines from London. In 1923 the Caledonian Railway became part of the newly formed London Midland & Scottish Railway.

For most of its 44-mile route from Stanley Junction (where the Highland Railway's main line branched off towards Inverness) to Kinnaber Junction the railway passed through fertile and undulating farmland with the only towns of any importance being Coupar Angus and Forfar. Locally generated traffic, much of it soft fruit in the summer, was therefore fairly light and closure of the whole route was recommended in the Beeching Report of 1963 with Glasgow-Perth-Aberdeen trains being diverted at Perth via Dundee and Arbroath.

Fortunately for railway enthusiasts the line from Perth to Aberdeen via Forfar in its final years became the stamping ground of Gresley's streamlined 'A4' Pacifics when they performed their swan song along the route in the 1960s. The end finally came on 4 September 1967 when all passenger services were withdrawn between Stanley Junction and Kinnaber Junction, with the line between Forfar and Bridge of Dun being closed completely. The section from Kinnaber Junction to Bridge of Dun and the Brechin branch retained a goods service until May 1981. The western section from Stanley Junction to Forfar kept its goods service until June 1982.

THE LINE TODAY

Armed with Ordnance Survey Landranger Maps Nos. 53 and 54 it is easy to follow the route of this line today. At Bridge of Dun the 4-mile branch line to Brechin, which closed to passengers in 1952 and to goods in 1981, was reopened in 1993 by the Brechin Railway Preservation Society. The stations at each end of the line have been restored and trains operate at weekends during Easter and in the summer months.

Southwest of Bridge of Dun the river bank next to the railway bridge over the River South Esk is a pleasant spot for a picnic, while a long section of trackbed southwest is now a farm track. Glasterlaw station, with its Caledonian Railway home signal, is now a private residence. Alongside the A932 near Guthrie the castellated entrance gate to Guthrie Castle cleverly disguises the railway embankment while, nearby, the station building and signal box at Auldbar Road are now part of a private residence. At Forfar the engine shed still stands, albeit in the industrial estate that now occupies the station site. West of Forfar the site of Glamis station, adjacent to the A928, is a pleasant spot complete with the remains of a goods loading dock. Part of the trackbed here is a forestry track.

Although very overgrown, the site of Alyth Junction, north of Newtyle, is still recognisable. The old station site at Coupar Angus, junction for the Blairgowrie branch, can only be described as 'Desolation Row' as it waits for the developers to move in. Finally, the major engineering feature on this line, the bridge over the River Tay at Ballathie, makes a fitting end to this railway odyssey through rural Angus and Perthshire.

Left *The line from Bridge of Dun to Brechin was reopened by a group of volunteers in 1993. The scene at Bridge of Dun today will delight all diesel enthusiasts.*

Above *Apart from the wheelie bins, the restored station at Bridge of Dun still exudes its Caledonian Railway heritage. Train rides up the 4-mile branch to Brechin operate during weekends in the summer.*

Above *Reminders of the past are everywhere. Many of the preserved locomotives are reminders of the 1960s diesel era on British Railways.*

Left *Brechin station terminus with its ornate London Midland & Scottish Railway sign in June 1962. Parked in front are two classic examples of British automobile engineering. Passenger services had ceased 10 years earlier but goods traffic up the branch from Bridge of Dun continued until May 1981. The station has since been restored and is now the westerly terminus of the Caledonian Railway (Brechin) Ltd.*

Above *An observant pair of eyes is always useful when tracing the remains of old railways. Here a sleeper and rail clips remain in situ near the bridge over the South Esk, southwest of Bridge of Dun.*

Below *A new use for the old railway bridge over the River South Esk. Here one of the original upright girders has been tipped on its side to provide a walkway for fishermen at this beauty spot.*

Below Swathes of rosebay willowherb and cow parsley line the old trackbed, now a farm track, between Bridge of Dun and Farnell Road station. It seems a million years ago that Gresley's 'A4' Pacifics thundered along here at the head of their three-hour Glasgow to Aberdeen expresses. By that time in the early 1960s, the stopping train service to rural stations like Farnell Road had long gone.

Left *This ex-Caledonian Railway home signal optimistically gives a clear road for the next train through Glasterlaw station. Complete with old level-crossing gates, the station is now a private residence.*

Right *Between Guthrie and Forfar the old station building and signal box at Auldbar Road are now part of a private residence. The railway bridge, an old platelayer's hut and the remains of a loading platform complete the scene. This section of line between Guthrie and Forfar was once part of the Arbroath & Forfar Railway. Although the railway was leased to the Aberdeen Railway in 1848 it retained its independence until the Big Four Grouping of 1923 when 120 railway companies around Britain were amalgamated into four large companies (GWR, LMS, LNER, SR).*

Below *The old railway line at Guthrie passed over the top of the main gate of the 15th-century Guthrie Castle – once home to the Clan Guthrie. The castle is now an upmarket wedding venue, which also boasts a nine-hole golf course in the grounds.*

Left *Forfar station with its curving platforms was once the junction not only for the Caledonian Railway's line to Dundee and secondary route to Brechin via Justinhaugh, but also for the Kirriemuir branch. Here, on a sunny 26 April 1952, a laundry basket belonging to Forfar Athletic Football Club awaits collection next to the Caledonian Railway lower quadrant home signal.*

Below *Despite its size Forfar engine shed was a sub-shed of Perth. Lined up outside on 26 April 1952 are, left to right, ex-LMS 'Crab' 2-6-0 No. 42738, an ex-LMS Stanier 'Black Five' 4-6-0 and two ex-Caledonian Railway 0-4-4 tanks. The latter were probably employed on the short Kirriemuir branch while the 'Crab', a product of Crewe Works in 1927, continued in service until 1964 when it was withdrawn from Stranraer engine shed.*

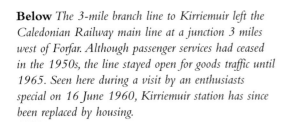

Below *The 3-mile branch line to Kirriemuir left the Caledonian Railway main line at a junction 3 miles west of Forfar. Although passenger services had ceased in the 1950s, the line stayed open for goods traffic until 1965. Seen here during a visit by an enthusiasts special on 16 June 1960, Kirriemuir station has since been replaced by housing.*

Right and right inset *The old station site and goods platform at Glamis is a pleasant spot next to the A928, half a mile north of Glamis Castle. The old trackbed under the double-track bridge leads back to Forfar. Glamis was once the terminus of the Newtyle & Glamiss Railway, which opened in 1838 and was absorbed by the Scottish Midland Junction Railway in 1846.*

Above *The site of Alyth Junction is slowly being taken over by nature. The junction once served trains on the Caledonian Railway main line and on the Dundee, Newtyle and Alyth line, which made a physical connection here. Passenger trains to Alyth ceased in the 1950s but goods traffic continued until 1965.*

Left *The goods-only line from Coupar Angus to Blairgowrie was visited by an enthusiasts special on 17 June 1962. Although passenger services had been withdrawn some years earlier, the terminus building and train shed were still in remarkably good condition. Set in a soft fruit-growing region the line saw seasonal traffic conveying harvested fruit to jam factories.*

Right *Car-makers Ford of Dagenham and Rootes of Coventry are well represented outside Blairgowrie's terminus building in June 1962. The timetables and posters are long gone – passenger trains had ceased a decade earlier.*

Above *The major engineering feature on the Caledonian Railway's main line between Perth and Forfar is the five-span viaduct across the River Tay near Ballathie. The river at this location is popular with fishermen.*

Right *Stanley Junction, seen here on 3 October 1946, was where the Caledonian Railway's main line from Aberdeen met the Highland Railway's main line from Inverness. Trains still operate on the latter route from Perth.*

GLENEAGLES TO BALQUHIDDER

Like many of Scotland's rural railways, the meandering line from Gleneagles to Balquhidder came into existence through the building of several independent lines during the 19th century.

First off the mark was the Crieff Junction Railway, which was authorised in 1853 to build the 9-mile line between Gleneagles, on the Scottish Central Railway's main line, to the town of Crieff. It was opened in March 1856 and absorbed by the Scottish Central Railway (SCR) in 1865. A few months later the SCR became part of the newly formed Caledonian Railway.

A second company, the Crieff & Comrie Railway, was authorised in 1890 to build a 6-mile line from the Caledonian Railway at Crieff to Comrie. Developed from a previously abandoned scheme to link the two towns the line opened on 1 June 1893. It was worked from the start by the Caledonian Railway, which eventually took it over in 1898.

The third scheme, to link Comrie with the Callander & Oban Railway at Balquhidder, got the green light in 1897 and was known as the Lochearnhead, St Fillans & Comrie Railway. Progress on the building of the line, the western half of which ran along the northern shore of Loch Earn, was slow and it opened in stages between 1901 and 1905. The Caledonian Railway agreed to operate it and subsequently took over the railway completely in 1902. Traffic was never heavy on this rural line and, despite the development of tourism around Loch Earn in the late 19th century, it never became profitable.

Long before Dr Beeching, the writing was on the wall for the Balquhidder to Comrie section and it closed to passengers in October 1951. The track was not immediately lifted and was

Left *This viaduct at Lochearnhead was built in 1904 to carry the Lochearnhead, St Fillans & Comrie Railway across the lower end of Glen Ogle. To the west, Lochearnhead station has been beautifully restored.*

Above *Still open for trains between Glasgow and Perth, the station at Gleneagles was the junction for the line to Crieff and Comrie. A four-wheeled diesel railbus waits to depart for Crieff on 11 June 1962.*

Above *Stanier 'Black Five' 4-6-0 No. 45492 waits to depart from Gleneagles with the 6.03pm to Crieff on 11 July 1957.*

Right inset *Closed in 1964, Muthill station has since been demolished. It is seen here from a Gleneagles to Crieff train in July 1957.*

occasionally used by goods trains in connection with the construction of the Breadalbane Hydro-Electric Power Scheme, which was completed in 1961.

Four-wheeled diesel railbuses were introduced in 1958 in an effort to reduce running costs on the remaining Comrie, Crieff and Gleneagles section. Sadly, this last-ditch effort did not save the line which fell victim to 'the Beeching axe' and was closed completely on 6 July 1964. Goods traffic was never heavy but Crieff continued to be served via the Almond Valley line from Methven Junction (closed to passengers in 1951) until 1967.

THE LINE TODAY

Gleneagles station is still open today and is served by trains on the Glasgow to Perth main line. Most of the route can still be followed using Ordnance Survey Landranger Maps Nos. 51 and 58.

Much of the route between Gleneagles, Crieff and Comrie has disappeared beneath farmland but cuttings and bridges at several locations, for example between Muthill and Highlandman, make our journey of discovery a lot easier. A public footpath now makes use of the trackbed along part of the route northwest from Auchterarder and between Strageath, near Muthill, and Crieff. The stations at Tullibardine and Highlandman (named after the cattle drovers

Right *Part of the trackbed of the line between Auchterarder and Tullibardine is now a footpath. Tullibardine station is now a private residence.*

who once stopped here) are now private residences but the large station site at Crieff has since disappeared beneath a car park and a housing estate. To the west of Crieff the route of the railway can still be traced along the north bank of the River Earn.

The road bridge over the railway on the eastern approach to Comrie is bedecked with flowers in the summer and the station site itself is now a caravan park. The scenery west of Comrie is magnificent and the trackbed and infrastructure of the line to Balquhidder is well preserved. Much of it can still be seen as it cuts through woodland alongside the A85. At St Fillans, where the line takes the northern shore of Loch Earn, the well-preserved station site, complete with station building, platform, waiting room and signal box is now part of a caravan park. Lochearnhead, with its magnificent concrete viaduct and beautifully restored station is the highlight of our journey. At Balquhidder, where the line from Comrie met the Callander & Oban Railway, the station site is now a caravan park but the grand frontage, complete with stone steps and subway entrance, are a well-known landmark by the side of the A84.

Table 32—continued

ABERDEEN, DUNDEE, PERTH, STIRLING, EDINBURGH (Waverley) and GLASGOW (Buchanan Street)

Week Days

Miles		am A		am ②	am E	am	am		am		am	am	am ② D		am	am	am	am
16	Aberdeen — — — dep											D		D	D			
30¾	Stonehaven — — —																	
42	Laurencekirk — — —															6 10		6 20
57¾	Bridge of Dun — — —															6 33		6 46
69¾	Forfar — — —															6 53		7
74	Alyth Junction — — —																	7 24
	Coupar Angus — — —																	7 50
35	Inverness — — — dep																	8 5
	Dundee (Tay B'dge) dep		ρ 11K20				ρ 11K20							MB Dundee to Glasgow				8 12
3¾	Dundee (West) — dep																	
10¾	Invergowrie — — —																	
20¼	Errol — — —											7 6						
20½	Perth (Princes St.) —																	
	Perth — — — arr											7 14			7 45			7 55
89½	Perth — — — dep		4 20									7 23						8 4
	Comrie — — — dep		4 33									7 38						8 14
	Crieff — — — arr / dep					6 30		7 0				7 40		8 14			8 31	8 32
	Pittenzie Halt — —																	
	Highlandman — —											7 45		8 16				
	Strageath Halt — —											7 57						
	Muthill — — —											7 58						
105¼	Tullibardine — —											8T						
117¾	Gleneagles — —											8T 2						
120	Dunblane — — —											8T 4						
122½	Bridge of Allan — —		5 5				6 54		7 24			8T15						
	Stirling — — — arr / dep		5 30				7 11		7 41			8 21			8 39			
131	Larbert — — — arr / dep		5 35				7 16		7 46		8 16			8 54				
			5 49				7 22		7 52		8 26				9 10			
			5 53				7 43		7 54		8 29							

Footpath

Footpath to
Strageath

Footpath to
Crieff 2½

Left, inset and above *Part of the trackbed between Strageath and Crieff is now a public footpath. A new halt at Strageath was opened on 15 September 1958 to coincide with the introduction of the railbus service. The halt had no platforms and passengers left and joined the train by way of folding steps.*

Above *Highlandman station, seen here on 15 June 1960, was named after the cattle drovers who once visited this area on their way to southern markets. Now a private residence, the building and platform have been beautifully restored, complete with nameboard and station clock.*

Left *During its final summer of operation on 2 June 1951, the 12.30pm Perth to Balquhidder train arrives at Crieff behind ex-LMS '4F' 0-6-0 No. 44251 and ex-Caledonian Railway 4-4-0 No. 54476. The '4F' was taken off here and the train then continued along the picturesque route on the northern shore of Loch Earn.*

Below *In the early summer of 1961 passengers leave the mid-morning railbus arrival from Gleneagles at the still-imposing surroundings of the station at Crieff, home of the famous Hydro hotel. Prior to closure in 1964, Crieff still enjoyed a service of up to 10 trains daily from the junction with the Perth–Glasgow main line at Gleneagles – evidently not enough to prevent closure. The railbuses were latterly replaced by steam haulage due to operational problems.*

Right *Stanier 'Black Five' 4-6-0 No. 45492 arrives at Crieff with the 6.03pm train from Gleneagles on 11 July 1957. In an attempt to reduce operating costs on the line these powerful main line locos with their two or three-coach trains were replaced by four-wheeled diesel railbuses just over a year later.*

Below *Easter 1966, just two years after closure, with the track not long lifted, the former Comrie station is already showing signs of decay. Originally part of the Caledonian Railway route from Perth through Crieff to Balquhidder on the Callander & Oban line, Comrie was the terminus of the 15-mile branch line from Gleneagles from 1951 to its July 1964 closure.*

Left *During June 1960 an enthusiasts special meandered its way around central and eastern Scotland visiting many soon-to-be-closed branch lines on its journey. Here, the train calls at Comrie on 15 June with its mixture of preserved, ex-LNER and BR carriages. The station site is now a caravan park.*

Right *The Lochearnhead, St Fillans & Comrie Railway opened between Comrie and St Fillans on 1 October 1901. Fifty years later to the day, the line closed to passenger services. High above Loch Earn the station site, including this original waiting room, is now a caravan park.*

Below *Drivers on the A85 from Crieff are welcomed in summer by this flower-bedecked railway bridge on the approaches to Comrie.*

Above *The preserved station at St Fillans, now part of a caravan park, still carries its original British Railways notice boards. Despite efforts in the early 20th century to publicise the railway for its scenic beauty and tourist potential, the line was never a financial success.*

Above and right *Ex-Caledonian Railway 4-4-0 No. 54476 heads out over Lochearnhead Viaduct with a train from Perth via Crieff on 2 June 1951 – just four months before the withdrawal of passenger services on this line. Built in 1904 the viaduct is the major engineering feature on this scenic route.*

Above *At the end of its journey from Crieff on 2 June 1951, No 54476 is turned manually at Balquhidder before returning with its lightly loaded train along the northern shore of Loch Earn.*

Above *The trains are long gone but the grand entrance staircase and subway tunnel at the site of Balquhidder station are easily spotted at the side of the A84 from Callander.*

DUNBLANE TO CRIANLARICH
AND LOCH TAY BRANCH

Eventually part of the through route between Dunblane and Oban, the Dunblane, Doune & Callander Railway was incorporated in 1846. Construction was slow to start and the 10½-mile line did not open until 1858. It was then leased to the Scottish Central Railway which itself was then absorbed by the Caledonian Railway in 1865. In that year the Callander & Oban Railway (C&OR) was incorporated but took 15 years before reaching its final destination. From the start, the line was financially backed by the Caledonian Railway which also agreed to work it. Construction through difficult terrain up Glen Ogle was very slow and Killin (later renamed Glenoglehead Crossing) was only reached in 1870. By 1873, the line had been extended to Crianlarich and a temporary terminus at Tyndrum.

Here construction work halted again for several years before pressing on to Dalmally which was reached in 1877. Beyond Dalmally the next obstacle was the Pass of Brander near Loch Awe. Oban was finally reached in 1880.

A 5-mile branch line from Killin Junction on the C&OR line to Killin and Loch Tay, incorporated as the Killin Railway in 1883, was opened in 1886. Crianlarich was later also served by the North British Railway's West Highland line to Fort William, which opened in 1894.

The opening of the C&OR certainly helped Oban to develop as a resort during Victorian times and, until 1964, a through sleeping car service operated during summer months from London Euston. The first closure came in 1939 when passenger services on the short Killin to Loch Tay section were withdrawn. Goods traffic continued with the small engine shed at Loch Tay

Left *With a 'Marie Celeste' atmosphere, the overgrown platform at Killin Junction is a vivid reminder today of Scotland's lost railway heritage. Out of the picture, the ruined station building is currently being restored as a private residence.*

Above *The railway line between Dunblane and Doune was doubled in 1902. Passing over this rusting bridge a short section of the trackbed east of Doune is a cycleway and footpath known as the 'Doune Trail'.*

Above *Callander was not only served by trains to and from Edinburgh and Glasgow each weekday but also a (summer only) sleeping car service to London Euston. Here, 'Black Five' 4-6-0 No. 45127 waits to depart with the 9.40am train to Edinburgh on 6 June 1963.*

remaining in use until total closure of the line. By the 1960s, rationalisation of services on the Oban line involved the complete closure of the Dunblane to Crianlarich Lower section and the Killin branch. Closure was planned for 1 November 1965 with Oban line trains being rerouted between Glasgow and Crianlarich via the West Highland line. In the event a serious landslip in Glen Ogle on 27 September brought this date forward and the line was never reopened.

THE LINE TODAY

Dunblane station is still open and served by trains on the Glasgow to Perth main line. Crianlarich Upper station is also still open and served by trains from Glasgow to Oban or Fort William. The route of the Dunblane to Crianlarich section is easily followed as much of it lies parallel to the A84 and A85 roads. Ordnance Survey Landranger Maps Nos. 51 and 57 clearly mark the route of the closed railway line. Both Doune and Callander stations have been demolished but a section of trackbed east of Doune is now a cycleway and footpath, as is a short section on the eastern outskirts of Callander. Here the large station site is now a car park but the cast iron road bridge over the site is still used by traffic. North of Callander the old trackbed has been transformed into a cycleway (National Cycle Network Route 7) along the western shore of

Loch Lubnaig and from Balquhidder up Glen Ogle, over the famous viaduct, finishing up in the village of Killin.

The station site at Balquhidder, with its impressive roadside entrance, is now a caravan park. An impressive view of the line up Glen Ogle and over the mountain-hugging viaduct can be had while driving north up the A85. With a 'Marie Celeste' quality the platform and ruined buildings at Killin Junction can be reached along what is now a forestry track which starts close to the junction of the A85 and the A827 to Killin.

Now descending gently down Glen Dochart the trackbed closely parallels the A85 and in places has disappeared altogether under road-widening schemes. Crianlarich Lower station has been demolished but a visit to the privately run tea rooms on the Upper station is a fitting end to our journey today.

Above and right *Built by J Cameron Arrol of Edinburgh, this bridge still carries road traffic across the east end of the Callander station site.*

Left *Between Callander and Strathyre the railway skirted the western shore of Loch Lubnaig. Today much of the trackbed from Callander to Killin has been transformed as part of National Cycle Network Route 7.*

Above *An Oban-bound train halts at Strathyre station on 18 June 1962. On the left is a camping coach and in front of the little timber signal box is an attractive water fountain topped by a heron partially hewn from granite from Ben Cruachan. Housing now occupies this site.*

Above *Strathyre's closed station and crossing loop, with the 2,693ft Benvane towering over Rob Roy country to the south. It is Easter 1966 and the track through the station – which had featured an attractive fountain sculpture of a heron – was lifted a year later. A similar heron sculpture survives at Dalmally station on the remaining section of the Callander & Oban line.*

Above *Balquhidder station on 2 June 1951. On the right the soon-to-be-withdrawn train to Crieff waits on the arrival of the connecting train from Oban before setting off along the shore of Loch Earn. Originally named Lochearnhead, the station was renamed Balquhidder in 1904 in readiness for the opening of the Lochearnhead, St Fillans & Comrie Railway.*

Below *Ex-Caledonian Railway 4-4-0 No. 54476 waits to depart from Balquhidder with the 2.25pm two-coach train to Crieff on 2 June 1951. An Oban-line train of 'blood and custard' coaches waits at the main line platform.*

Right *Today the grand staircase and subway entrance to Balquhidder station lead nowhere. The station site is now a caravan park.*

Table 32—continued

OBAN, BALLACHULISH, KILLIN, STIRLING, EDINBURGH (Waverley) and GLASGOW (Buchanan Street)

Week Days only

Miles from Oban	Miles from Ballachulish			am	am	am	am	am	am	am	pm S	pm	pm S		pm D	pm	pm DE	pm E	pm S	pm S	pm S
									9 10		1145		12 5	1240		4 55	5 15	5 35		6 57	9 20
—	—	Oban .... dep			6 15		8 25			10 48				4 15				7038		
—	—	Ballachulish Z .... dep				7 14				10 53				4 16				7 14		
2	—	Ballachulish Ferry				7 20				10 59				4 18				7 18		
8½	—	Kentallen				7 36				11 22				4 41				7 21		
14½	—	Duror				7 46				11 29				4 5				7 25		
17½	—	Appin				7655				L				5				7 31		
24¼	—	Creagan				8 11												7 34	8 59	
27	—	Benderloch				8												7038	9 36	
		North Connel			6 30	8 208 49	9 25		11 54	12		1226		5 115	17 5 28	5 47	8 13	9 20	
6¼ 27½		Connel Ferry ... {arr			6 30	8 208 49	9 25		11 54	12		1226		5 115	17 5 28	5 47	8 13	9 20	
		Connel Ferry ... {dep			6 31	8 288 59	9 26		12 2			1233			5 48	6 36	8 18		
9¼		Ach-na-Cloich			6 45		9 33					1240				6 31			
13		Taynuilt			6 52		9 41		1215			1249				6 35			
22		Loch Awe			7 29		10 5									6 42			
24½		Dalmally			7 42		10 12									6 45			
36¼		Tyndrum Lower			8 2		10 40												
41½		Crianlarich Lower			8		10 54												
48		Luib					11 5												
		Killin .... dep			7 55		9 56 1054								7 187 23				

Miles from Killin																				
		Killin Junction {arr			8 8		1010 11 7 1113								7 24				
5¼ 4½		(Exchange Platform only) {dep			8 15		1114								7 40				
51¾		Balquhidder			8 31		1129								7 46				
59½		Kingshouse Platform			8034		1136												
60½		Strathyre {arr			8 40		1149												
62¾		Strathyre {dep			8 56		1155												
70½		Callander {arr		7 52	9 6	9 40	12p7			2 59				8 33				
		Callander {dep		8	9 6	9 54	1217	1 44		3 19				8 58				
78½		Doune		8 16	9 27	10 3		1 54						9 25	1019	1025		
82		Dunblane {arr			9 39	1011		1230		2 29		4 31	6 56		9 33			
						1016		1 28		2 44		4 33	8 1					
						1 19		3 3		3 30		5 30						
87		32Stirling		8 26	9 39	1011		1230									
123½		32Edinburgh (Waverley)		9840	1116	1016		1 28									
117½		32Glasgow (Buchanan St.)		9 13	1028	1 19		3 3									

Notes / References:

B	Change at Larbert and Polmont
b	Stops to take up when passengers on platform. Luggage and bicycles not dealt with
D	Diesel Service
E	Except Saturdays
F	Upper Station
L	Calls on notice to set down or take up
MB	Miniature Buffet Car
N	Stops to set down only on notice at Connel Ferry
n	noon
p	pm
Ø	Calls at Barcaldine Halt
RC	Restaurant Car
S	Saturdays only
SC	Sleeping Car
TC	Through Carriages
X	Arr Glasgow (Queen Street)
Y	Calls at Falls of Cruachan on Saturdays to take up on notice at Taynuilt
Z	Ballachulish is the station for Glencoe and Kinlochleven
Ⓐ	Second class only

Column heading notes: TC Oban to Glasgow · TC Oban to Edinburgh · TC Oban to Edinburgh except on Saturdays from 13th July · RC Oban and Glasgow · TC Oban to Glasgow · RC Oban to Edinburgh · Commences 11th July · TC Oban to Glasgow · TC Oban to Glasgow and Edinburgh · MB Observation Car Oban to Stirling · SC and RC Oban to London (Euston) and to London arr Kensington (Olympia) · SC Oban to London · RC Oban to Glasgow · TC Oban to Glasgow and Edinburgh · Arr Ballachulish · Arr Oban · TC Callander to Edinburgh · TC Callander to Glasgow · TC Callander to Glasgow

Above *Headed by British Rail Standard Class 4 2-6-4 tank No. 80126 a mixed-train departs from Killin Junction to Killin on 6 June 1963. The line was closed on 27 September 1965 after a landslip in Glen Ogle brought about the earlier-than-planned demise of the Callander & Oban route between Dunblane and Crianlarich.*

Left *Construction of the Callander & Oban line was slow and took 15 years to reach its destination. Difficult terrain in Glen Ogle slowed progress while this 12-arch viaduct was built. It now carries National Cycle Network Route 7.*

Below *Birmingham Railway Carriage and Wagon Company Type 2 D5358 leaves Killin Junction with the 9.30am Oban to Glasgow while British Rail Standard Class 4 2-6-4 tank No. 80093 awaits departure with the 11.27am to Killin on 4 August 1965.*

Above *Killin Junction at Easter 1966. When the photographer and his family walked across the moor to the junction on holiday from Edinburgh, they found a scene reminiscent of the 'Marie Celeste'. Everything was intact, and the station log book lay open at the last entry before a landslip in Glen Ogle permanently closed the line between Callander and Crianlarich on 27 September 1965.*

Below *British Rail Standard Class 4 2-6-4 tank No. 80093 waits to depart from remote Killin Junction with a one-coach train to Killin on 4 August 1965. Reached along forest tracks, the island platform still exists today.*

Right *Killin Junction station served only one purpose – as an exchange platform for the Killin branch. Railway staff at this lonely posting were once housed in this now derelict cottage.*

Below *To the east of Killin Junction passengers on the train to Killin were afforded far-reaching views across Glen Dochart. Part of the trackbed on the lower section of this branch is now used by National Cycle Network Route 7 into Killin village.*

Below inset *Diminutive ex-Caledonian Railway 0-4-4 tank numbered as LMS No. 15103 heads a Killin branch train on 28 July 1931.*

Above *Steam superpower for a one-coach train – British Rail Standard Class 4 2-6-4 tank No. 80093 runs around its train at Killin after arriving from Killin Junction on 4 August 1965. Built at Brighton in 1954 this loco was withdrawn in September 1966.*

Below *Built in 1886, ex-Caledonian Railway 0-4-4 tank No. 15103 halts at Killin on its journey from Loch Tay to Killin Junction on 28 July 1931. Passenger services between Killin and Loch Tay were withdrawn in 1939.*

Above *The end of the line at Loch Tay in August 1965 – the tiny engine shed is just beyond the closed station which by then was a private residence. No. 80093 is returning to Killin after taking on fuel at the shed. Less than two months later this delightful branch line had closed.*

Left *Ex-CR 0-4-4 tank No. 15103 takes on water at Loch Tay engine shed in July 1931. Until 1939 trains ran to a pier at Loch Tay station to connect with passenger steamers on the loch.*

Above *From Killin Junction the Callander & Oban line turned westwards down Glen Dochart to Crianlarich. Remains of the line, such as this small bridge over a stream near Luib, can be spotted alongside the A85. Once a passing loop, Luib station site is now a caravan park and campsite.*

Right *Kathleen Casserley, wife of the famous railway photographer Henry Casserley, shelters from the rain at Crianlarich Lower station on 25 July 1931. Beyond the station is the viaduct that carries West Highland line trains from Glasgow to Fort William. Trains to Oban now run from Glasgow Queen Street via the West Highland line route to Crianlarich Upper where they rejoin the original Callander & Oban route westwards.*

EAST FIFE:
LEUCHARS JUNCTION TO THORNTON JUNCTION

Until the building of the Tay and Forth railway bridges in the late 19th century, railway development in the county of Fife was hampered by poor links with the rest of Scotland. Despite this drawback, by the mid-19th century proposals for railways to link the Fife coalfields and the important fishing industry along its long coastline had been put forward.

The coastal route from Leuchars to Thornton started life when the St Andrews Railway from Leuchars Junction to St Andrews opened in 1852. This railway was absorbed by the North British Railway (NBR) in 1877 but remained a branch line for the next 35 years.

The approach from the west started in 1854 when the Leven Railway from Thornton to Leven opened in 1854. It was worked from the outset by the Edinburgh, Perth & Dundee Railway (EP&DR) which linked the passenger and goods ferries across the Firths of Forth and Tay. The EP&DR was absorbed by the NBR in 1862. In 1857 the East of Fife Railway extended the coastal line from Leven to Kilconquhar.

The Leven Railway and the East of Fife Railway were reincorporated as the Leven & East Fife Railway in 1861, extending the coastal line from Kilconquhar to Anstruther in 1863.

The missing link between Anstruther and St Andrews was only completed in June 1887 by the opening of the Anstruther & St Andrews Railway. Worked from the outset by the NBR, the line was amalgamated by that company on 1 August 1897. The railway map of East Fife was completed in 1898 by the opening of the goods-only East Fife Central Railway from East Fife Junction, between Cameron Bridge and Leven, and Lochty.

The opening of the Forth Bridge in 1890 led to a rapid development of the Fife coast as a favourite destination for holidaymakers from the industrialised central belt. Through trains from

Left *The trackbed at Kilconquhar is now a footpath. This section of line opened from Leven in 1857 and was extended to Anstruther in 1863. Closure came on 6 September 1965.*

Above *Ex-NBR 4-4-0 'D30/2' No. 62418 'The Pirate' waits to depart from Leuchars Junction with the 2.17pm Dundee to Edinburgh via St Andrews on 8 September 1955. Leuchars Junction is still open.*

Glasgow and Edinburgh to resorts such as Pittenweem, Anstruther and Crail continued to run during the summer until the 1960s. However, competition from road transport and a reduction in UK-based holidays led to the closure of the line between St Andrews and Thornton on 6 September 1965. The remaining branch line from Leuchars to St Andrews closed in 1969, as did Thornton Junction station. The western section between Thornton and Leven and the branch to Methil remained open for freight (mainly coal for export and distillery traffic) until the end of the 20th century. There are now plans to reopen the 5-mile section from Thornton to Leven and link passenger services with the current Fife Circle Line.

THE LINE TODAY

Leuchars station is still open and well served by trains between Edinburgh and Dundee. Still visible are the piers of the old railway bridge over the mouth of the River Eden at Guardbridge. The station site at St Andrews is now a car park. Stravithie station, nearly 2 miles north of the village it served, has been restored and is in use as a country guest house complete with a British Railways Mark 1 carriage in the grounds. Boarhills station is now a private residence, while, near Kingsbarns, a long stretch of trackbed with overbridges is now a cycleway and footpath towards Crail. Old stations have many uses and

part of Crail station site is no exception as it is now a garden centre. Anstruther station has disappeared. Further west both Pittenweem and St Monans stations are private residences. The trackbed west of the Kilconquhar station site is now a footpath to Lower Largo. The engineering highlight on the line is Largo Viaduct, which lies to the west of the station site, now a car park. Very little remains of the goods-only branch line to Lochty, which opened in 1898 to serve collieries and farms. Three years after closure in

Above 'B1' 4-6-0 No. 61263 leaves St Andrews with a Dundee to Glasgow Queen St relief on 7 August 1965. The Fife coast line closed one month later.

1964, the terminus of the line became the headquarters of the 1½-mile Lochty Private Railway and, for a while, was home to 'A4' Pacific No. 60009 'Union of South Africa'. The line closed in 1992 but traces of the yard and trackbed at Lochty can still be seen today.

Above *Ex-NBR 4-4-0 'D30/2' No. 62418 'The Pirate' waits to depart from St Andrews with the 2.17pm Dundee to Thornton Junction train on 8 September 1955. The line from here to Thornton closed 10 years later.*

Above *During the last summer of operation on the line, 'B1' 4-6-0 No. 61263 bursts from under a road bridge near Mount Melville with a Dundee to Glasgow Queen Street relief on 7 August 1965. Only 18 years old when seen here, the 'B1' was withdrawn from Dundee Tay Bridge engine shed at the end of 1966.*

Left and right *Stravithie station is now a country guest house. Set in the landscaped station site a British Railways Mark 1 carriage is also used for accommodation.*

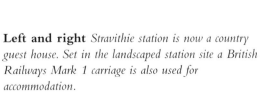

Above *Not long before its 1965 closure, passengers wait to board an afternoon St Andrews to Edinburgh train at Crail's neat station and crossing loop on the single-track Fife coastal line. Latterly Crail had just four passenger trains a day, but one was a through service from Glasgow Buchanan Street, reflecting the traditional holiday attraction of the 'East Neuk' for Glaswegians.*

Right *Near Kingsbarns, a long stretch of trackbed with overbridges is now a cycleway and footpath leading towards Crail. This section of line to Boarhills opened in September 1883.*

Left *A sunny day in September 1955 as a Dundee to Thornton Junction train calls at Pittenweem station. Those were the days when carriage windows could be opened during hot weather.*

Right *British Rail Standard Class 4 2-6-0 No. 76109 enters Elie with the 4.51pm Thornton Junction to Anstruther train on 7 August 1965 – there are no passengers in sight. The station closed one month later. Only eight years old when seen here, the locomotive was withdrawn a year later.*

Below *'B1' 4-6-0 No. 61404 enters Pittenweem with the 8.37am Thornton Junction to Crail train on a sunny 7 August 1965.*

Above *During the summer months the Fife coast was served by through trains to and from Glasgow and Edinburgh. Here, in its last summer of operation, 'B1' 4-6-0 No. 61103 passes through Kilconquhar with the 3.30pm Crail to Glasgow Queen Street on 7 August 1965.*

Left *Apart from this small bridge parapet and signal wire pulley nothing much now exists of the railway at Kilconquhar. The trackbed west of here is a footpath to Lower Largo.*

Right *The attractive viaduct at Lower Largo is the only major engineering feature on the Fife coastal line. The Fife Coastal Path passes through here on its 90-mile route between the Tay Bridge and the Forth Bridge at North Queensferry.*

Above '*B1*' *4-6-0 No. 61330 enters Cameron Bridge with the two-coach 2.42pm Crail to Thornton Junction train on 6 August 1965. The line between Thornton and Leven remained open to serve a distillery at Cameron Bridge and a coal-export facility at Methil until the end of the 20th century.*

Above *The Fife coastal line met the main line between Dundee and Edinburgh at Thornton Junction. The large engine shed here not only provided motive power for the Fife coastal line but also for the many collieries in the area. To cope with increasingly heavier coal trains, the North British Railway's ubiquitous J36s were augmented with the more powerful J37s, 104 of which were put into operation between 1914 and 1921. Here is No. 64570 reposing in the depot yard at Thornton Junction in the summer of 1965.*

Left and below *The East Fife Central Railway was authorised in 1893 to build a goods-only line from Fife Central Junction (between Cameron Bridge and Leven) and Lochty. The company was amalgamated by the North British Railway three years before opening in 1898. A planned extension to the Fife coastal line at Kingsbarns was never built. Three years after closure in 1964, the terminus of the line became the headquarters of the 1½-mile Lochty Private Railway and, for a while, was home to 'A4' Pacific No. 60009 'Union of South Africa'. The line closed in 1992 but traces of the yard and trackbed at Lochty can still be seen.*

Below *A section of the summer 1964 timetable for trains between Edinburgh and Dundee and the Fife coastal line.*

WAVERLEY ROUTE:
EDINBURGH TO CARLISLE

The famous Waverley Route from Edinburgh to Carlisle had its beginnings in a horse-drawn tramway that linked collieries southeast of Edinburgh to Leith Docks. Known as the Edinburgh & Dalkeith Railway it opened in stages from Leith to Dalkeith between 1831 and 1838.

Although nominally independent the Edinburgh & Hawick Railway was originally financed by directors of the North British Railway (NBR) and was transferred to that company in 1845. The railway ran from South Esk (north of Newtongrange) to Hawick and opened throughout in 1849. The NBR soon had its eyes on reaching Carlisle and in 1859 the Border Union Railway was authorised to extend the Edinburgh & Hawick route across the border into England. Attempts by the London & North Western (L&NWR) and Caledonian Railways (CR) to stop the NBR entering Carlisle were

thwarted when the latter entered the city by leasing the Carlisle & Silloth Railway & Docks Company. Despite heavy engineering works through bleak and sparsely populated country the line to Hawick opened in 1862. The Waverley Route was now complete.

However, continuing disputes with the L&NWR and the CR at Carlisle rumbled on and it wasn't until 1876, when the Midland Railway opened its Settle & Carlisle line, that the Waverley Route started to make economic sense. For the first time passengers could now travel from London to Edinburgh without using either the East Coast or West Coast main lines. Although intermediate traffic between the isolated communities along the route was negligible the Waverley Route was a useful alternative to the east and west coastal lines and also carried important Anglo-Scottish freight traffic. Motive power for the line came from the NBR engine

Left The 15-arch Shankend Viaduct carries the Waverley Route over the Langside Burn, a tributary of Slitrig Water, 5½ miles south of Hawick. Now a Grade B listed structure the viaduct is the responsibility of BRB (Residuary) Ltd.

Above Ex-NBR Class 'J35' No. 64479 heads out onto the Waverley Route from the Dalkeith branch at Glenesk Junction on 21 April 1960. The Dalkeith branch, part of the Edinburgh & Dalkeith Railway, a horse-drawn tramway, was opened in 1838.

Left *Reopening of the Waverley Route between Edinburgh and Tweedbank is due in 2013. Land along the route is currently being purchased by Transport Scotland prior to the rebuilding of infrastructure and track laying. Compulsory purchase notices, such as this one north of Stow, are now a familiar sight.*

Above and right *BR Sulzer Type 4 'Peak' D19 heads the 10.15am Edinburgh Waverley to St Pancras express ('The Waverley') across Lothianbridge Viaduct, Newtongrange, on 6 June 1964. The viaduct, with its 23 arches alongside the A7 near Newtongrange south of Edinburgh, is a fine example of Victorian railway engineering. Built in 1847 this impressive structure will soon carry trains again on the new Waverley Railway.*

LOTHIAN BRIDGE CARAVAN PARK 0131 663 6120

sheds at Edinburgh St Margarets and Carlisle Canal. Four smaller engine sheds at Riccarton Junction, Hawick, St Boswells and Galashiels provided engines for local work on branch lines to Peebles, Selkirk, Reston, Jedburgh, Reedsmouth and Hexham.

Introduced as the 'Thames–Forth' express in 1927 and renamed in 1957 the most important train of the day over the Waverley Route was 'The Waverley', which ran between London St Pancras, Carlisle and Edinburgh Waverley. Travelling via the scenic Settle & Carlisle line the train took more than nine hours to reach its destination – three hours longer than the fastest train on the East Coast main line in the 1960s. This handicap led to the train's withdrawal in September 1968.

The uneconomic Waverley Route became one of the longest lines in the country to be listed for closure in the Beeching Report of 1963. Despite strong objections from the public and local MPs, closure was planned for 15 July 1968. Although delayed by a few months so that alternative road transport could be arranged the end came on 5 January 1969. Protesters had the last word, however, as the final train to traverse the line –

the 21.55pm sleeper from Edinburgh Waverley to London St Pancras – was halted at Newcastleton until the early hours of 6 January by local people who blocked the level-crossing gates. Despite closure the track remained in situ until early 1970 while a consortium calling itself the Border Union Railway tried to purchase the line from British Rail. Its bid was unsuccessful and by mid-1972 all track south of Millerhill had been lifted and the Waverley Route ceased to exist.

THE LINE TODAY

The closure of the Waverley Route in 1969 led to Galashiels, Melrose and Hawick becoming the most isolated towns in the UK. For 30 years this isolation has severely restricted growth in the Borders but a feasibility study published in 2000 showed that reopening the line between Edinburgh and Tweedbank, near Melrose, would deliver major economic and social development opportunities to the area. In June 2006 the Waverley Railway (Scotland) Bill was passed by the Scottish Parliament by 114 votes to 1 with one abstention. The project was transferred to Transport Scotland in August 2008 with the

Above *More than 40 years since closure the concrete platform at Heriot station awaits the reopening of the Waverley Railway between Edinburgh and Tweedbank in 2013.*

reopening of the line – at a cost of £300 million – scheduled for 2013.

Much of the infrastructure of the Waverley Route still exists and the line can be easily traced today using Ordnance Survey Landranger Maps Nos. 66, 73 and 79. South of Edinburgh, Lothianbridge Viaduct with its 23 arches alongside the A7 near Newtongrange is a fine example of Victorian railway engineering. Built in 1847 this impressive structure will soon carry trains again on the new Waverley Railway. Much of the Waverley Route between here and Galashiels is easily traced to the west of the A7 as road and railway parallel each other down the

Below *South of Hawick the Waverley Route climbs the valley of Slitrig Water to the curving 15-arch Shankend Viaduct. This Grade B listed structure has recently been repaired and waterproofed by BRB (Residuary) Ltd. The company is responsible for about 3,800 bridges, tunnels, viaducts and other structures on closed railway lines throughout the UK.*

valley of Gala Water. Numerous railway bridges can be spotted as the railway crosses and recrosses the river 15 times in as many miles. North of Bowland the short Bowshank Tunnel is still in very good condition.

At Galashiels the 5-arched Redbridge Viaduct over the River Tweed is now a listed structure maintained by BRB (Residuary) Ltd. Also at Galashiels a large retaining wall, built after a landslip in 1916, and the short Ladhope Tunnel will soon see railway activity again. Tweedbank, midway between Galashiels and Melrose, is to be the site of the new terminus station for the Waverley Railway. At Melrose the A6091 bypass has been built on the trackbed of the railway for a couple of miles and drivers along this stretch of road now have a good view of the preserved station, platform and canopy. Little now remains of St Boswells station but the engine shed and a platform can still be traced.

South of Hawick, where the station site has long gone, the railway climbs the valley of Slitrig

Water through Stobs to the curving 15-arch Shankend Viaduct. This fine, listed structure has also recently been repaired and waterproofed by BRB (Residuary) Ltd. South of the viaduct, the privately owned Shankend station and signal box can be clearly seen on the high embankment to the west of the B6399. The line then veers westwards through a large area of forestry plantations before plunging into the depths of Whitrope Tunnel and emerging at the summit of the Waverley Route at Whitrope Sidings. The tunnel, nearly ¾-mile long, is the fourth longest in Scotland but access is now blocked due to a roof collapse at the southern end in 2002.

Whitrope is now the headquarters of the Waverley Route Heritage Association, which has laid a short length of track from Signal Box Cottage to the cutting south of the tunnel mouth. From the car park here it is possible to walk south along the trackbed for two miles through forestry plantations to the eerily silent Riccarton Junction. Inaccessible by road,

Riccarton Junction is one railway pilgrimage worth making. Here the island platform has been partially restored with station nameboard and a (disconnected) red telephone box. A few ruined railway buildings, including the former NBR schoolhouse, still remain. A short length of recently relaid track and an old goods guards van complete the picture. To the south the trackbed leads through more forestry plantations to Steele Road where the former station building is now a private residence.

From Steele Road the railway and the B6357 snake down the valley of Liddel Water through Newcastleton where the former station house marks the spot of the famous closure protest of 5–6 January 1969 (see page 145). Less than three miles to the south is the border with England where the route of the line can be followed through Kershope Foot, Riddings, Scotch Dyke and Longtown to the outskirts of Carlisle.

Right *Immediately to the south of Shankend Viaduct was Shankend station, signal box and sidings. Both these buildings are now private residences. Heavy southbound freight trains were often banked from here up to the summit of the line at Whitrope. Just under 18 months before closure, the station is seen here from a southbound train on 12 July 1967.*

Below *The British Railways summer 1964 timetable for the Waverley Route.*

Above *Between Heriot and Galashiels the Waverley Route crosses and recrosses Gala Water 15 times in as many miles. This bridge north of Stow is one of many that can be seen today alongside the A7 trunk road.*
By 2013 it is hoped that trains on the new Waverley Railway will once again travel along this scenic route.

Above *Seen here on 28 April 1952, Galashiels was also the junction for trains to Peebles and Selkirk. The site is now a car park and Station Brae overbridge and the station building have recently been demolished.*

Right *At Melrose the A6091 bypass has been built on the trackbed of the railway for a couple of miles and drivers along this stretch of road now have a good view of the preserved station, platform and canopy.*

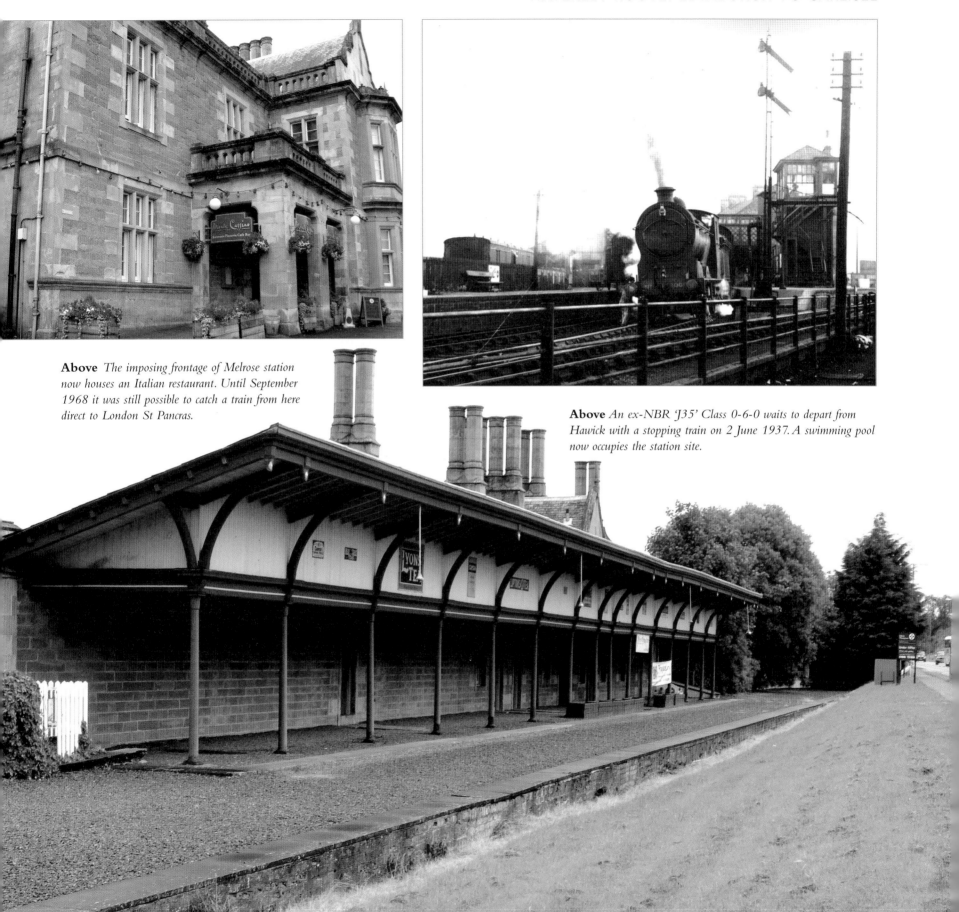

Above *The imposing frontage of Melrose station now houses an Italian restaurant. Until September 1968 it was still possible to catch a train from here direct to London St Pancras.*

Above *An ex-NBR 'J35' Class 0-6-0 waits to depart from Hawick with a stopping train on 2 June 1937. A swimming pool now occupies the station site.*

Above and right *The summit of the Waverley Route was at Whitrope Sidings. A short length of track has been laid here by the Waverley Route Heritage Association which has its headquarters at Signal Box Cottage. The summit-marker post is also a memorial to Henry (Harry) Jardine who was an engine driver on the line for 47 years.*

Left *At nearly ¾-mile long, Whitrope Tunnel is the fourth longest railway tunnel in Scotland. Access is now barred by this metal fence due to a roof collapse at the southern end in 2002.*

Below *Class 'A2' Pacific No 60532 'Blue Peter' heads an enthusiasts special at Whitrope Summit in October 1966. Designed by Arthur Peppercorn, this fine loco was built in 1948 and withdrawn in December 1966. It has since been preserved.*

Above *Set amid vast tracts of forestry land, this LNER concrete stile still stands next to the trackbed north of Riccarton Junction.*

This picture *With no road access Riccarton Junction was a self-contained community – everything came in and went out by train. A branch of the Hawick Co-operative Society, seen here in April 1952, was located on the island platform.*

Above *The arrival of a train at Riccarton Junction in 1955 attracts interest from some of the local children. Until 1963 children of railway staff were educated at the nearby railway-owned school.*

Left *The trackbed of the Waverley Route south of Whitrope Sidings. The Waverley Route Heritage Association hopes to reopen the line between Whitrope and Riccarton Junction.*

Above *This postcard shows Riccarton Junction in 1907. During its heyday more than 100 people lived and worked at this lonely outpost, which had its own school, post office and grocery shop. Doctors travelled by train from Newcastleton or Hawick to visit patients. The branch line to Kielder and Hexham closed in 1956.*

Left *The island platform at Riccarton Junction was restored by the Friends of Riccarton Junction in 2004. A short length of track, station nameboard and red telephone box complete the picture.*

Right *Seen from inside a stranded guard's van, the former generator building was restored by the Friends of Riccarton Junction as heritage centre.*

Above *Ex-NBR 'J35' 0-6-0 No. 64509 simmers outsde the coaling plant at Riccarton Junction on 28 April 1952.*

Above *By 1966, the writing was on the wall not only for the Waverley Route but also for steam traction. Here two of the infamous and short-lived Clayton Type 1 diesels, D8570 and D8578, struggle through Steele Road towards Riccarton Junction with a northbound goods train in June of that year.*

Left *Newcastleton, seen here in July 1967, was the setting of the famous closure protest when locals, angered by the closure of the Waverley Route, padlocked the level-crossing gates and blocked the line on the night of 5–6 January 1969. The final train from Edinburgh was delayed by several hours before it could proceed on its journey.*

Left *The vast site of Riccarton Junction is now owned by the Forestry Commission. The only buildings that remain here are the roofless shell of the stationmaster's house, seen here on the left, and the old schoolmaster's house further up the hill. The latter has been converted into a private residence.*

Right *Just over the border in England, Riddings Junction, seen here on 16 April 1953, provided connections to the Langholm branch, which was opened by the NBR in 1864. Passenger trains ceased in June 1964 and the line was closed in September 1967.*

INDEX

PHOTOGRAPH ACKNOWLEDGEMENTS

All modern-day colour photographs by Julian Holland.

t = top; b = bottom; m = middle; l = left; r = right

W J V Anderson: 64*t*

H. C. Casserley: 10*b*; 11*tl*; 11*bl*; 15*tr*; 19*tr*; 19*bl*; 20*tl*; 23*b*; 25*tr*; 28*b*; 32*bl*; 32*br*; 33*br*; 36*tl*; 39*tr*; 41*tl*; 43*t*; 43*b*; 45*tr*; 45*br*; 47*b*; 48*tl*; 50*tl*; 52*t*; 52*b*; 53*t*; 53*mr*; 53*bl*; 56*tl*; 59*br*; 60*mr*; 62*tl*; 64*mr*; 66*tl*; 66*bl*; 67*tr*; 68*tl*; 80*t*; 81*t*; 81*b*; 83*b*; 86*t*; 86*b*; 87*br*; 88*b*; 89*tl*; 89*mr*; 89*bl*; 92*tl*; 93*bl*; 98*tl*; 98*mr*; 98*bl*; 100*ml*; 100*br*; 101*br*; 103*b*; 104*t*; 105*tr*; 107*b*; 108*tl*; 109*tr*; 110*tl*; 112*bl*; 113*tr*; 116*tl*; 119*tr*; 120*t*; 120*b*; 123*t*; 126*bl*; 127*b*; 128*bl*; 129*br*; 131*b*; 132*br*; 136*tl*; 147*tr*; 148*bl*; 149*tr*; 153*tr*; 154*tr*; 155*m*; 155

Derek Cross: 155*t*

John Goss: half title; contents page; 91*b*; 123*b*; 124*b*; 127*t*; 128*t*; 132*t*; 133*t*; 136*b*; 137; 138*t*; 140*t*

Tony Harden: 10*tl*; 69*b*; 153*tl*; 153*mr*

Derek Huntriss: 151*b*

Ian Macmillan: 38*tr*

Milepost 92½: 140*b*

Ivo Peters Collection: 19*br*

W. Sellar: 55*b*; 58*bl*; 143*b*; 144*tl*

David Spaven: 71*br*; 76*t*; 76*b*; 80*b*

Frank Spaven: 12*tl*; 17*tr*; 18*bl*; 19*ml*; 24*tl*; 31*tr*; 33*t*; 40*t*; 43*tr*; 64*tl*; 79*br*; 108*b*; 109*b*; 119*b*; 124*t*; 134